T0062055

CRYSTALS
SIMPLIFIED

CRYSTALS SIMPLIFIED

13-Digit ISBN: 978-1-64643-369-8
10-Digit ISBN: 1-64643-369-6

This book may be ordered by mail from the publisher. Please include $5.99 for postage and handling. Please support your local bookseller first!

Books published by Cider Mill Press Book Publishers are available at special discounts for bulk purchases in the United States by corporations, institutions, and other organizations. For more information, please contact the publisher.

Cider Mill Press Book Publishers
"Where good books are ready for press"
501 Nelson Place
Nashville, TN 37214

Visit us online!
cidermillpress.com

Typography: Essonnes, Sweet Sans Pro

Printed in China

All vectors and images used under official license from Shutterstock.com.

1 2 3 4 5 6 7 8 9 0
First Edition

CRYSTALS
SIMPLIFIED

THE GUIDE TO SPELLCASTING, HEALING, MEDITATION, AND SPIRITUAL WELL-BEING

ISABELLA FERRARI

CIDER MILL
PRESS

BOOK
PUBLISHERS

CONTENTS

CHAPTER ONE
WHAT IS A CRYSTAL?
8

CHAPTER TWO
HEALING CRYSTALS
30

CHAPTER THREE
FIFTY CRYSTAL PROFILES
52

CHAPTER FOUR
SPELLS, RITUALS, AND
CRYSTAL GRIDS
140

INTRODUCTION

As people living in the modern age, we all face many challenges, from climate change to political crises and beyond. This is why people are rediscovering the importance of spirituality and self-care as a daily practice: the art of taking care of the body, mind, and soul. The need for spiritual connection has caused crystals to rise in popularity, capitivating many across the globe.

Although you might think of crystals as a new tool that Mother Earth has offered us, in truth, crystals have been used for their powers for thousands of years. Their vibrating colors, various shapes, and powerful abilities have led many people to include them in their spiritual practices, but also to use them as ornaments for the home.

We might know the most common crystals, like amethyst, rose quartz, or obsidian, and some might disregard the less common ones, those with dull colors and rough shapes. But the attributes of all crystals are the same; they are effective and powerful, versatile enough to be used in all spiritual paths and magickal practices ("magick" with a k is distinct from "magic," which refers to the mundane tricks of magicians). We're lucky to have access to all types of crystals, including those that were undiscovered until recently. Their extremely high vibrations and impressive ability to help us to connect with our higher selves and improve our lifestyles are only some of the many positive uses of crystals. In the following chapters, we will review how we can use crystals as an offering, a tool to manifest what we desire, a way to create a positive environment, and as a gift for our loved ones.

As my primary practice is under the umbrella of folk-based rituals, I will also share with you how you can incorporate crystals into an earth-based magickal practice. I'd like this book to function as a guide for all people, regardless of religion, belief, and practice. I'd like you to take from this book anything that might be useful for you and improve your life, no matter what path you're following.

Crystals are a tool that our planet has kindly gifted us; they contain the beautiful powers of the universe, which are limitless. In the first part of this book, we will learn about how they form, their different colors and sizes, how to use them, and how to take care of them. You will then find a detailed list of some of the many crystals you can use and study. Finally, I will share some rituals and spells you can perform with these powerful tools.

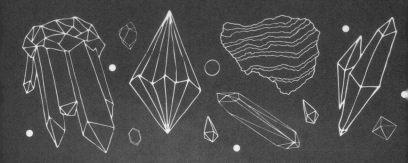

CHAPTER ONE

WHAT ARE CRYSTALS?

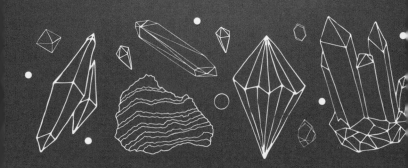

A crystal is a solid material formed by atoms arranged in a definite pattern and with a geometrically regular shape.

Each type of crystal has an "identity" formed by a unique internal arrangement of atoms that determines the mineral's chemical and physical aspects, such as color. With this information, we know that, by observing a crystal's structure under a microscope, we can identify it. Some crystals might appear very different in shape and color but in reality have the same structure. Therefore, they are the same type of crystal.

The formation of crystals is known as crystallization, which comes from ancient Greek; it means "iced" and "rock crystals." The term indicates the creation of a crystalline structure from a fluid or other materials dissolved in a liquid, or, more rarely, from gas. Some crystals can be formed by the same mineral or combination of minerals, but each type will have a different crystallization. As many atoms are added over time, a crystal continually grows in melted rock and waters rich in minerals or vapor.

Beneath our planet, we can find a molten material called magma. A very thin layer of it has cooled, forming a crust. Inside this crust, the mineral-rich magma continues to boil, forming new crystals.

Some crystals form at a superheated temperature that makes them rise to the surface of our planet—for example, quartz. As gases enter the crust, they cool and solidify as they meet solid rock; if this process is slow, the crystal can grow big. If the process is relatively fast, then the crystal will be small.

Many alternative formations might also occur. For instance, a crystal like obsidian is formed by an extremely fast process; a very high temperature forms aventurine from liquid magma; tourmaline is formed by gases penetrating adjoining rocks; calcite forms through an erosion process; garnet and other similar crystals are formed by minerals melting and recrystallizing under high temperatures and pressure.

When we talk about these many different types of crystals, we might encounter different and confusing terminologies, like "mineral," "rock" (or "stone"), "crystal," and "gemstone." Although many people use these terms as synonyms, and I myself tend to use some of them interchangeably, they differ in technical definition.

MINERAL: A mineral is a naturally occurring solid with a specific chemical composition and crystalline structure. They can form on the surface when solutions containing dissolved minerals evaporate, beneath the surface when dissolved elements leave a hot water solution, or when materials melt in magma, then cool down and solidify.

ROCK: A rock is made out of many minerals and organic materials. A combination of heat and pressure creates blocks of stones, like granite or marble. Some things that are called crystals are, in reality, stones, like lapis lazuli.

CRYSTAL: A crystal is a solid material in which atoms are arranged in a definite pattern; they are comprised of no more than one mineral.

GEMSTONE: A gemstone is a precious or semi-precious mineral that has been cut and polished and is usually used as jewelry.

There's more to crystals than just the fascinating scientific processes that make them. Since our species has discovered them, they have been amazing us with their intriguing aspects and incredible spiritual power. Their internal geometry reflects the many different shapes they can have. Not only are these shapes beautiful to the eye; they have different spiritual meanings and usage. Every shape has different vibrations and will elicit varied emotions.

Let's dive into the shapes you will find when looking at crystals:

POINT

The naturally pointed shape perfectly directs your energy where you want it to go.

If you are performing a spell, use a pointed crystal to direct your energy to an object or person; if you're practicing manifestation, write down your goals on a piece of paper, fold it, and place the crystal on top of the paper. The pointed crystal will send the energy out in the universe and will help you achieve your aspirations.

SPHERE

A crystal sphere emits energy from all points. It is a perfect representation of our planet and the circle of life: birth, life, death, and rebirth.

You can hold a crystal sphere in your hand while meditating. For example, selenite and amethyst are ideal for this purpose. We can use this crystal shape to practice scrying, the art of getting answers by looking into a mirrorlike surface. In this case, you might want to choose crystals with a "glassy" appearance like quartz or obsidian.

PYRAMID

Pyramids were considered a powerful shape for populations like the ancient Egyptians; the apex of a pyramid was seen as a way to connect with spirits and the divine.

This shape can be a manifestation tool to intensify your energies and intention.

HEART

A heart-shaped crystal is not in its natural form, as it has to be polished into this form; however, this doesn't prevent it from having incredible energy and radiating love, empathy, and compassion.

This shape is ideal for working on our Heart chakra and love spells. While holding it, we can imagine our heart being filled by its light rays, feeling a great sense of calm and pure love.

CUBE

A cube-shaped crystal is best if you need to feel grounded and connected with the Earth.

Its shape will stabilize your emotions and make you feel more balanced. You can also place a cubed crystal in each corner of a room to protect it from negativity and unsettling energies; amethyst or black tourmaline are definitely good choices for this purpose.

EGG

The egg is the symbol of fertility and birth; it can be used in fertility spells but also to encourage new beginnings or whichever new aspect or project we want to welcome into our life.

WORRY STONE

A worry stone has the shape of a smooth disk. It is advised you use it for meditation and absorbing energies. You can either hold it in your hands or rub it between your fingers. Its vibrating energies will calm you and make you feel at peace.

RAW

A raw crystal is a crystal that hasn't been shaped by human hands. Its shape is natural, and it hasn't had many interactions with humans. For this reason, some believe that it has higher vibrations, and that the energies are far more powerful. This hasn't been proved, so it is up to you if this shape resonates more for you or not.

WAND

A wand is a crystal that has been shaped to have a pointed end and a long body. It is used to direct energy; a pointed crystal like clear quartz can also be used as a "battery" to recharge other crystals. You just have to put your quartz in the middle of a plate and place your other crystals around it for a whole night or even the entire day.

DOUBLE POINT

A crystal with two pointed ends will simultaneously send energy in two different directions. You can use it during a ritual to invite love, harmony, balance, peace, and more.

CLUSTER

As you might expect, a cluster is a group of crystals that naturally grow together. The set of pointed crystals all together will radiate enormous and beautiful waves of energy that will fill your room with positive energies. It is advised you keep them in your living room or in the middle of the dining table to bring all the people that live with you together in a peaceful atmosphere.

HOW TO PICK A CRYSTAL?

Often, we might feel lost and confused when it's time to buy a crystal. Sometimes we just feel the need to bring a new crystal into our home, and other times we might have a specific purpose, like relieving our anxiety or bringing more peace into our life; either way, it can be overwhelming to figure out what crystal to buy after seeing the enormous variety the market offers us.

If we try to see crystals as an active source of energy, almost as entities or spirits, we should surely value how we feel when we are with them. Many people pick their crystals by focusing on the feelings and sensations they experience when holding them. Building a relationship with a crystal and getting to know its energy and how it communicates that to you is extremely important when you want to form an opinion on a specific stone.

The physical experience, however, might not always be possible. Likely, your local crystal shop won't always have the specific stone or gem you're interested in, as it is almost impossible for a business owner to sell all of them. That's why online shops, much of the time, are a good choice when we have a specific type of crystal in mind; in this case, we can only make our decision based on the crystal's appearance and maybe some customers' reviews.

However, by buying online, we risk getting a crystal that doesn't feel right in person; its energy might not resonate well with us. The same can happen if a crystal is gifted to us. When we are in this particular situation, we don't have to panic or feel demoralized. Sometimes it only takes a good cleansing practice to fix the problem, and we will talk more about that in the upcoming section (page 21).

That said, there are still some tips we can use to narrow down our choices when buying a crystal.

THE SIZE

In the crystal world, the size of a stone doesn't indicate how powerful or helpful the stone is going to be. Size does not matter, as it's only important regarding how you'd like to use the crystal. If you'd like to place it in your living room to decorate a table and bring specific aspects into your home, a more significant size could be the right fit for you. If you would like to carry a crystal with you throughout the day, then a smaller size that could fit in your bag or wallet might be the best choice. Remember that what is most important is the fusion of your energy and intentions with the crystal's vibrations and power.

THE SHAPE

As mentioned previously, each shape has a different use and vibration. The shape changes the vibrations of a crystal and our sensory experience. When we think about buying a crystal, we have to think about why we're buying it and the sensation we would like to feel. Getting a tumbled, smooth stone in the shape of an egg or heart will give us a significantly different sensation than a raw stone. That's why it's crucial to pick the shape carefully, as it will affect our practice.

THE COLOR

With crystals, every color has its own association; the meaning of each color is often taken from esoteric practices or the chakra system. Following these practices, every color will represent different aspects of your physical, emotional, and spiritual sphere. The color of a crystal doesn't tell you all about that crystal, but it can help direct you to the right one.

The primary color associations we might find in the spiritual world include the following:

WHITE: healing, connection with the divine, cleansing

BLACK: protection, grounding, warding off negativity, introspection

ORANGE: strength, exploring sexuality, success, making art

RED: passion, sex, taking initiative, courage, determination

GREEN: personal growth, money, abundance, luck, fertility

BLUE: clear communication, clarity, empathy, healing

PURPLE: intuition, spiritual self, psychic ability, wisdom, truth

YELLOW: confidence, creativity, ambition, joy, independence

BROWN: comfort, home, connection with animals

CLEAR: universal clarity, amplifying intentions, purification

PINK: love, self-compassion, friendship, gentleness, romance

GRAY: calm, peace

These are the main aspects to take into consideration when we're ready to buy a new crystal. Although they are significant, remember that your feeling while holding a crystal is the most important. If you have a sense of emptiness and don't feel the right connection, that means that that specific crystal is not meant for you.

All these tips together will direct you to your perfect crystal; a good crystal choice will, without a doubt, bring much positivity into your life, boost the power of your spells, and help you reach your goals.

PICK YOUR CRYSTALS ETHICALLY WHEN POSSIBLE

The practice of mining crystals and the industry's impact on our planet is undoubtedly an essential topic for those who care about the environment. A wise choice when shopping can undeniably make a difference in your efforts to protect the Earth and the people on it. Where a business gets its crystals from and how the miners are protected are extremely important elements to consider.

Secondhand crystals are also a very valid option. Many people don't feel comfortable buying an already-used crystal, as it might contain remnants of others' energies. But if we consider how long a crystal takes to form (it can take millions of years!), a good crystal cleansing is the perfect solution to "clean" our crystals and use them again.

The more we follow this simple procedure, the more we, crystals lovers, can make a difference and never stop actively caring about our home, planet Earth.

CRYSTALS CLEANSING AND CARE

Crystals absorb the energy that's around them. If you use a crystal for your healing practice or spell, the healing crystal will absorb the energy that is present in that situation. The same happens when we carry a crystal with us, or we leave it somewhere untouched. No matter the situation, crystals are an energy sponge, so cleansing them is essential.

Cleansing a crystal will eliminate all the energies that it is storing, making it vibrate as it should again. There are various cleansing methods that you can pick when it's time to cleanse your stones:

SMOKE

Using the smoke of an incense stick or smudging herbal bundles is an excellent cleansing technique. Let the smoke touch your stone by passing it above your incense. While doing it, imagine your crystal expelling all its energies. You will probably see people cleansing their crystals with sage, as it is becoming increasingly popular in the spirtualistic community. Always remember that this herb and ritual comes from Native American and Indigenous people. Try to be respectful of their practices when using this herb.

WATER

Leave your crystal in a bowl of water for several hours. The water will slowly absorb the crystal's energies, cleansing it thoroughly. Before picking this cleansing technique, double-check that your crystal can withstand it, as many crystals cannot be in contact with water. Generally, you should only water-cleanse crystals that are a 6 or above on the Mohs Hardness Scale.* In addition, iron ores such as pyrite, magnetite, and so on (as a general rule, the majority of crystals that end in -ite) will rust in water. It's important to state that these are just general rules, and that there are exceptions; always make sure to do your research.

SALT

Salt is a great tool to absorb unwanted energies and cleanse ourselves. The same can be said of crystals. Burying our stones in salt is an excellent cleansing method to eliminate any negativity. As with water, salt can potentially ruin our crystals and corrode them. Any crystal that is lower than a 7 on the Mohs scale cannot be placed in salt. Crystals that are above 7 are safe in salt and saltwater.

SNOW

If you live in a cold place, or during winter, burying your crystals in snow will allow the snow to change the energies of the stones from negative to positive. Don't pick this cleansing technique for crystals that cannot be in water.

CRYSTALS

Some crystals have the power to reset other crystals' energy by touching them. The most popular crystal for this practice is selenite. Leaving one of your crystals touching selenite overnight will cleanse its energy, and the crystal will be ready to be used again.

*IN 1812, FRIEDRICH MOHS INVENTED A SCALE THAT REPRESENTS MINERALS' HARDNESS, WHICH IS THE CRYSTAL'S RESISTANCE TO BEING SCRATCHED.

In addition to these cleansing methods, you can always ensure that your crystals are clean and well taken care of. If you're not displaying them in any particular place in your house, wrap them in a velvet or silk cloth. By doing so, you will protect them from being scratched and ruined.

Polish your crystals every so often so they don't get dusty. You could also give them a special place, exclusively for them, like a box or drawer; this way, they won't be surrounded by external vibrations.

All these activities will strengthen your relationship with your crystals and help you understand them more.

When we go beyond the barrier of seeing our crystals only as a physical body and start looking at them as living spirits, we will not only bond with them, but it will feel more natural to protect them and discover their powerful magick.

CHARGING CRYSTALS

Charging your crystals is another great practice when working with them.

Think of a crystal as a battery: every so often, its energy needs to be recharged to work effectively and help you achieve results. Their energy source is the natural world surrounding us—by following some basic charging methods, your crystals will have fresh and new energy.

- MOONLIGHT: The full moon is such a great source of power for our crystal companions. Leave them under the moonlight overnight. You can place them outside your window or in your garden if you have one.

- QUARTZ POINTS: Place your crystals on a flat surface. Surround them with three or more (I like to pick odd numbers) quartz crystals pointing inward. Leave them there for several hours; the quartz will channel positive energy, and your crystals will be ready to be used again.

- PENTACLE: If you have a pentacle disk, place your crystals in the middle of it. You can also draw one on a piece of paper, or you can draw your own sigil. Either of these magickal symbols will charge your stones and renew their energy.

- VISUALIZATION: Hold your crystal in your hands. Go into a meditative state and focus on your energy. Imagine a white source of light coming from your heart, passing through your arms and hands and into your stones. Your energy will charge your crystals and give them new power.

• PLANTS: Place your crystals in your plants' pots or under a tree where the crystal can touch the tree's root or barks. It is crucial to pick healthy, thriving plants. This way, their vibrant energy will be passed into your stones.

• HERBS: Some herbs have the power to renew your crystals' energy. You can, for example, burn them and use the smoke as an energy source. Or you could boil the herbs in water, let the water cool, and immerse your crystals in it for several hours. The most common herbs for this practice are mugwort, St. John's wort, rosemary, and sage.

PROGRAMMING YOUR CRYSTALS

Programming your crystals is another excellent way to benefit from their power, and it's very different from cleansing and charging them.

Programming a crystal is giving a stone a specific task; it's almost like you're giving them an assignment. Doing so will channel their energy to a specific aspect of your life or a particular goal you'd like to achieve.

You can infuse many intentions into your stones: attracting a new love, manifesting your dream job, or protecting your physical and spiritual body from external energies. When you want to program a particular crystal, follow the following steps:

1 Cleanse and charge the crystal.

2 Ground yourself and go into a meditative state; be entirely focused on this ritual.

3 Hold the crystal in your hand. Focus your attention on your energy and the crystal's vibrations.

4 Have a clear intention. Try to be very specific when thinking about your goal.

5 Say it out loud or whisper it to the crystals. Depending on your feelings, you can repeat the same sentence more than once.

6 Think of your goal as if it's already happening. Visualize the stream of light that is your intention going into the crystal. Feel the emotions and enjoy every feeling.

7 Your crystal is now programmed, filled with the power of your intention.

After your crystal is cleansed, charged, and programmed, it's ready to support you in your manifestation journey, whatever your goals and dreams are. Following these three steps is a powerful practice that will strengthen your bond with your crystals. Every time you touch or see your stone, you will feel the incredible energy it holds and sends out to the universe.

Match these rituals with concrete actions to achieve your goals, and your manifestation practice will get a boost of positive energy from your crystal companions; they will help you bring positivity, fulfilment, and joy into your daily life, and their magick will make your home a magickal place.

WHAT DO I DO IF MY CRYSTALS BREAK?

A broken crystal can be a valid reason for stress and sadness. When one of our stones gets ruined or breaks into pieces, it can be a hard pill to swallow.

However, this might not always be a negative event. It is essential to analyze the situation and understand what was happening when the crystal broke. You might have been having an argument with someone, going somewhere, or perhaps making an important decision. When a crystal breaks, it is evident that the crystal and the universe are trying to send us a message.

It could mean that the crystal has done its work and it's ready to be back with Mother Earth; it could be a sign that you must pay attention to what's surrounding you and the decisions you're making; or it could just be too old, and its presence will no longer serve you. This is why when we're presented with a completely broken crystal, although it's hard, it's time to let go of its energy and presence.

If the crystal is chipped, and we're unsure of what to do, we should always spend some time meditating with the crystal and feeling what its energy is like. Sometimes a good cleansing is all that is needed to restore our crystal's vitality.

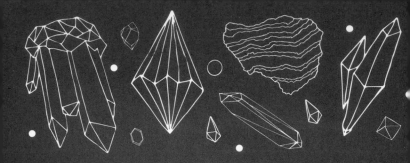

CHAPTER TWO

HEALING CRYSTALS

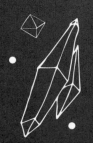

Crystal healing is an ancient practice that uses crystals and other stones to cure and prevent diseases and physical and mental problems.

The use of crystal healing goes back to at least 6,000 years ago, to the Sumerians of Mesopotamia; they were the first population to use crystals like lapis lazuli or carnelian to ward off negativity and illness.

Each crystal has a different vibration with specific characteristics that are able to aid our physical and spiritual bodies. Not only that, but some crystals are known to have minerals with great therapeutic properties. Malachite, for example, is excellent for aching muscles and preventing infections. Lapis lazuli is a perfect ally for migraines and headaches; however, if the headache is caused by stress or anxiety, then placing amethyst on your brows might help you soothe those feelings. Even medical practices and machines use crystals because some (like quartz) are piezoelectric—this means that electricity and sometimes light can travel through them when they are compressed.

We can also learn from ancient healers and shamans that pressing a crystal wand on our skin, on the specific part of our body that needs to be healed, will send a healing ray to relieve the pain. Ancient healers were very aware that while many crystals have specific healing powers, others have the ability to calm and stimulate at the same time.

Stones like magnetite can calm an overactive organ and energize an underactive one. Some crystals will help you heal your blockages more quickly, while others have a slower healing process. A calming crystal that will tranquilize your emotional sphere and stimulate your self-love is rose quartz. On the other hand, one of the most powerful crystals you can touch is moldavite, which stimulates spiritual awakening, clears energy blocks, and connects you to your Higher Self.

HEALING PRACTICES

Now that we have learned how crystals can heal our body, mind, and soul, we can dive deeper into the healing practices we can perform to use our powerful companions.

The reasons we practice crystal healing are many: we might have a slight physical pain caused by overloading ourselves, we may feel stress, or there has been a sudden change of temperature and weather. We could have emotional blockages that keep us from feeling happy and at peace, a broken heart after a breakup, or general stress at work or as a result of feeling like we are at a crossroads in our life, which are all valid reasons to feel unbalanced and unaligned with the universe. Our internal conflicts, chaotic thinking, and constant worries will eventually manifest themselves through bodily pain and emotional distress.

In modern society, there is an incongruence between how normal it is to visit the doctor when we have a physical disease and strange it might seem to do the same for our spiritual body when it is suffering. Giving care to ourselves as living beings includes nurturing every single aspect of who we are, and that's why crystal healing can be a great practice to incorporate into our routine.*

*CRYSTAL HEALING IS NOT A SUBSTITUTE FOR MEDICAL TREATMENT, BUT A SPIRITUAL SUPPLEMENT. PLEASE ALWAYS FOLLOW YOUR DOCTOR'S ADVICE.

Let's explore the main healing practices:

CHAKRAS HEALING

The chakras are an ancient model that originated in India and represent different parts of our bodies that hold key energy centers. The word "chakra" comes from Sanskrit, and it means "wheel" or "disk." Visualize them as spinning wheels that receive and send different spiritual, physical, and emotional energies.

Along our spine, we have seven chakras, corresponding to different organs and nerve bundles in our body. The aim is to open and unblock them in order to realize our fullest potential as magickal beings. Most of us, especially those who don't practice any spiritual activity, might have one or even all of the chakras closed. This will cause us to experience an unbalanced life, with physical pain and mental instability, all related to the characteristics of the specific affected chakra.

For thousands of years, crystals have helped to cleanse and clear our chakras. Here I will introduce each of the seven chakras and the crystals you can use in relation to them:

THE ROOT CHAKRA

Starting from the bottom we find our first chakra, the Root chakra, also called *Muladhara* in Sanskrit. It is located at the base of our spine, at the pubic area in front, and at the tailbone at the back. The Root chakra is powerfully related to contact with the Earth, and with the ability to feel grounded and have solid roots. It is responsible for feelings of safety, stability, confidence, and the ability to manifest.

The four petals that form its symbols are related to four aspects of our consciousness: mind, intellect, consciousness, and ego. The square represents stability and the triangle represents the Earth, which reminds us of grounding.

SIGNS OF A BLOCKED ROOT CHAKRA: anxiety, instability, inability to enforce boundaries, poor immune system, feeling of frustration

SIGNS OF AN UNBLOCKED ROOT CHAKRA: security, stability, positive mindset, rational thinking

COLOR: red

ELEMENT: earth

BODY PARTS: hips, legs, lower back, sexual organs

MANTRA: Lam

CRYSTALS TO USE: garnet, bloodstone, red jasper, black tourmaline, tiger's eye, smoky quartz, hematite

THE SACRAL CHAKRA

The second chakra is the Sacral chakra, also called *Svadhisthana* in Sanskrit. It is positioned two inches below the navel and is the center of our pleasure and creativity. It holds our need for sexuality, connection with our inner child, intuition, and self-worth. It's highly connected with being friendly and fearless in expressing ourselves. It is also influenced by how we managed our emotions during childhood.

The six lotus petals represent the six aspects we have to overcome to purify this chakra: anger, jealousy, cruelty, hatred, pride, and desire. The circles represent birth, death, and rebirth, while the crescent moon represents chaos and endless change.

SIGNS OF A BLOCKED SACRAL CHAKRA: inability to let go, emotional instability, manipulation, tension, being withdrawn, low or overactive libido

SIGNS OF AN UNBLOCKED SACRAL CHAKRA: passion, creativity, ability to flow with emotions, sensuality, gentleness, flexibility, fluidity

COLOR: orange

ELEMENT: water

BODY PARTS: sexual organs (women), kidneys, bladder, large intestine

MANTRA: Vam

CRYSTALS TO USE: amber, citrine, peach moonstone, coral, carnelian agate, orange calcite, imperial topaz

SOLAR PLEXUS CHAKRA

Our third chakra is the Solar Plexus chakra, also known as *Manipura* in Sanskrit. We can find it in the upper abdomen, just below the breastbone in the center of our stomach. Our third chakra is where our warrior self dwells. It represents strength, ego, passion, power, and ambition. It is also what makes us experience astral travels and connection with our spirit guides.

The ten petals represent our ten currents of energies and vibrations called *pranas;* the reversed triangle indicates the three lower chakras spinning upward toward the higher chakras.

SIGNS OF A BLOCKED SOLAR PLEXUS CHAKRA: lack of motivation, lack of confidence, confusion, worry about what others think, anxiety, poor digestion

SIGNS OF AN UNBLOCKED SOLAR PLEXUS CHAKRA: feeling empowered, motivated, cheerful, outgoing, confident, healthy immune system, self-respect

COLOR: yellow

ELEMENT: fire

BODY PARTS: stomach, small intestine, liver, pancreas

MANTRA: Ram

CRYSTALS TO USE: tiger's eye, topaz, malachite, yellow jasper, yellow jade, citrine

 HEART CHAKRA
The fourth chakra is the Heart chakra, *Anahata* in Sanskrit; as the name suggests, it is located in the center of our body, in the heart space. It is the epicenter of our love, compassion, spirituality, and joy.

The Heart chakra allows us to love others and ourselves, to give and receive without expectations. It is also in this part of our body that we hold a considerable amount of pain; let's think, for example, of when we are heartbroken or deeply hurt.

Carrying this emotional pain is also called having heart scars; when we are able to release our heart scars, we remove all the pain we are holding, and we allow our hearts to heal.

The twelve lotus petals symbolize the twelve divine qualities of our heart: love, bliss, peace, harmony, understanding, empathy, purity, clarity, compassion, unity, forgiveness, and kindness.

The two triangles forming a hexagram are the female and male energies blending together.

SIGNS OF A BLOCKED HEART CHAKRA: distrust of others, feeling sorry for yourself, unworthy, jealous, judgement, afraid of letting go, negative self-image, respiratory issues

SIGNS OF AN UNBLOCKED HEART CHAKRA: feeling compassionate, empathetic, peaceful, able to forgive, inner peace, kindness, good blood pressure and circulation

COLOR: green

ELEMENT: air

BODY PARTS: chest and heart (physically and emotionally)

MANTRA: Yam

CRYSTALS TO USE: rose quartz, kunzite, green

aventurine, watermelon tourmaline, jade, green calcite, malachite, amazonite

THROAT CHAKRA

The fifth chakra is the Throat chakra, also called *Vishuddha* in Sanskrit. It is located above the collar bone, in the neck, and it's where our voice, our truth, flows from the inside out into the world. It is also where our anger is stored and where we can let it go. The Throat chakra is connected to communication, authenticity, creativity, transformation, and the possibility of change and healing.

The sixteen petals are the sixteen Sanskrit vowels, which are very easy to pronounce, which signify the airy quality of communication. This is why a blocked Throat chakra makes communicating very difficult. The inverted triangle represents a channel to our soul body, and the circle is a full moon, a symbol of a purified mind.

SIGNS OF A BLOCKED THROAT CHAKRA: inability to express yourself, quietness, timidity, weakness, inability to listen, inability to enforce healthy boundaries, misunderstanding, sore throat

SIGNS OF AN UNBLOCKED THROAT CHAKRA: feeling balanced, being a good speaker, listening skills, inspiration, decisive actions

COLOR: blue

ELEMENT: space

BODY PARTS: neck, throat, teeth, ears, thyroid glands

MANTRA: Ham

CRYSTALS TO USE: lapis lazuli, blue topaz, aquamarine, azurite, turquoise, angelite, blue lace agate

THIRD EYE CHAKRA

Our sixth chakra is the Third Eye chakra, also known as *Ajna* in Sanskrit. We can find it in the center of our forehead, above our eyebrows. Here is where we tap into our psychic powers and deepest intuition. It is also where we can get rid of negative tendencies and selfish behaviors. The Third Eye chakra holds intuition, energies of spirits, light, and spiritual awareness.

The two petals are the sense of duality between the self and God. The inverted triangle is your connection with the divine and enlightenment.

SIGNS OF A BLOCKED THIRD EYE CHAKRA: inability to focus, distrust in your decisions, fear of success, selfishness, lack of creativity

SIGNS OF AN UNBLOCKED THIRD EYE
CHAKRA: intuition, clarity, telepathy, astral travels, inner wisdom, imagination, no attachment to material things

COLOR: indigo

ELEMENT: command center of the elements

BODY PARTS: eyes, face, brain, lymphatic and endocrine systems

MANTRA: Ham or Ksham

CRYSTALS TO USE: amethyst, sodalite, lapis lazuli, purple fluorite, azurite, blue apatite, black obsidian

 CROWN CHAKRA
The last of the seven chakras is the Crown chakra, called *Sahasrara* in Sanskrit. It is located at the top of the head and is the center of spirituality, cosmic greatness, the highest vibrations, and enlightenment. It is connected to the Goddess, our pure energy. It helps us find our spiritual well-being and deepest wisdom. The Crown chakra is also the place where the soul comes into our body at birth and leaves at death.

The thousand lotus petals show our connection with the divine; the lotus flower represents prosperity and the eternity of these connections. The circle is a full moon, a symbol of the awakening of the conscious mind.

SIGNS OF A BLOCKED CROWN CHAKRA: confusion, lack of joy, insomnia, nightmares, destructive feelings, frustration

SIGNS OF AN UNBLOCKED CROWN CHAKRA: access to the unconscious and subconscious, wisdom, clarity, feeling connected to the universe, lucid dreaming, acceptance

COLOR: purest white or violet

ELEMENT: beyond the elements

BODY PARTS: head, mind

MANTRA: Om

CRYSTALS TO USE: diamond, clear quartz, amethyst, Oregon opal, labradorite, selenite

AURA HEALING

When we think about our bodies, most of the time we picture a physical one, tangible and visible. But there is, in reality, so much more beyond our tangible body—and that is the aura. The aura is a subtle biomagnetic sheath that surrounds our physical body. It can expand from eighteen inches to three feet from our body and contains all the information regarding our physical, mental, spiritual, and emotional health. Every single physical living body has this field of light surrounding the body.

Think of the aura as a bubble made out of several layers (also called bodies or planes). Each layer holds different information and a specific color.

Each layer interacts and relays information through our seven chakras and the external environment. Our thoughts, emotions, health, awareness, and past experiences are stored in different layers. Apart than representing your well-being, these layers influence your way of feeling, thinking, and acting. That's why we can use the size and thickness of the aura's layers and chakras to determine many aspects of someone's personality and current situation.

One of the most common questions regarding this topic is: *What is the difference between the aura and the chakras?*

The biggest difference is that the aura's colors change based on the person's feelings, moods, and intent, while the chakras are deeply rooted in us and take more time to change. Only big events and extensive internal work can change the state of our chakras. We can therefore say that the chakras are more internally placed, while the aura is external.

Although some believe there are a dozen layers forming our aura, there are certainly seven main ones:

1. **ETHERIC LAYER:** This is the closest layer to our physical body, half an inch to two inches from our skin. It's connected to the physical condition and health of our body. It is connected to the Root chakra and its color can vary: a more grayish color for active people and blueish for passive people.

2. **EMOTIONAL LAYER:** This layer can extend from one to three inches away from the body. It is connected to our emotions, feelings, and sensitivity. Because it is connected to our emotional state, this layer can often change. It is connected to the Sacral chakra and it can be all the colors of the rainbow, although it gets muddy when we experience stressful and dark emotions. This layer has a lot of impact on our chakras.

3. **MENTAL LAYER:** This layer lies outside the emotional layer and it exists three to eight inches from the physical body. It is connected to our thought processes, which can include our logical process, ideas, consciousness, belief system, rules, judgment, etc. It's connected to the Solar Plexus chakra and its color is yellow. Usually, it is brighter and sparkling when someone engages in an activity, creative situation, or in those who have an overactive mind.

4. **ASTRAL LAYER:** This is where the group of layers connected to our physical body ends and those connected to our spirituality begins, representing a bridge between the two. This layer can be eight to twelve inches away from the physical body. It is involved in forming our astral connection with others. Here we can find our sense of love, balance, and connections. It is related to the Heart chakra and the color is a pink-rosy shade. It gets stronger during loving and balanced relationships and weaker during breakups and disputes. This layer can also represent the state of our seven chakras.

5. **ETHERIC TEMPLATE LAYER:** This layer is the blueprint of your physical body on the spiritual plane. It lies about two feet away from the physical body. It represents what you create on this level, which can be your personality, your identity, and your general energy. It is connected to the Throat chakra and can vary in color. It gets much stronger when you know who you really are.

6. **CELESTIAL LAYER:** This layer can extend to two and a half feet away from the physical body, and it's known to be the layer of unconditional love. It shows our subconscious mind and it's affected by spiritual practices, devotion, and the

process of enlightenment. It is representative of our spiritual journey and our connection with the divine. It is related to the Third Eye chakra and its color is pearly white.

7. SPIRITUAL OR KETHERIC LAYER:

Depending on our spiritual state, this layer can extend from three to five feet away from our physical body. It vibrates at a higher frequency and protects all the layers. It holds all the information about your soul and previous lives. It represents you being one with the universe and it is the blueprint of your spiritual path. It is connected to the Crown chakra and psychic abilities and its color is bright white or golden.

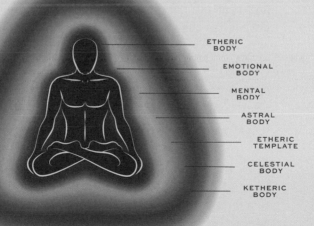

ETHERIC BODY

EMOTIONAL BODY

MENTAL BODY

ASTRAL BODY

ETHERIC TEMPLATE

CELESTIAL BODY

KETHERIC BODY

The layers that form our aura are not visible to everyone. However, when someone gives us "bad vibes" or we experience specific feelings when we are near someone, that is a signal coming from their aura. You might find reiki practitioners, holistic healers, or other spiritual individuals that are able to see your aura and guide you to heal the different layers.

Of course, the healing process can be aided by our crystals; through their specific and powerful qualities we are able to cleanse, purify, and protect our aura's layers.

You will find a more in-depth explanation of crystals' healing capabilities in chapter three (page 52). However, here is a quick list of some of the crystals you can use for aura healing, which you might practice by holding the crystals or by laying down and placing them on your body in relation to the affected chakras:

AMBER: aligns the aura and clears negative energies

AMETHYST: heals the holes in our aura and protects it

BLOODSTONE: considered a great etheric cleanser

CITRINE: cleanses, aligns, and fills the gaps in the aura

FLUORITE: supports a psychic shield

LABRADORITE: protects our aura and prevents energy leaks

MOONSTONE: cleanses your aura and balances vibrations

SELENITE: cleanses your aura and gets rid of unwanted vibrations

QUARTZ: increases the auric field and protects our aura

MEDITATION WITH CRYSTALS

Meditation is probably one of the most common practices to get to know our crystals better and practice self-care. During this practice, we have the opportunity to clear our mind from all the thoughts, worries, and distractions that our daily life can bring. It is a moment of relaxation where we can tune in with ourselves and embrace our spirituality. When we meditate with a crystal we open the door to the crystal's energies, allowing the crystal to communicate with us and giving ourselves the chance to understand how we truly feel with that crystal.

There are different ways you can meditate with a crystal: Some people like to pick one crystal at a time and do a full session of meditation while holding it.

Others prefer to select more than one crystal, sometimes picking seven different crystals whose colors correspond to the colors of our seven chakras.

This last method will increase the vibrations and might make you feel overwhelmed or extremely joyful. This is why it is always important to feel grounded, balance our emotions, and maintain a certain level of concentration. To do so, you could decide to meditate with fewer crystals or include the calming effect of other stones.

Here is a simple guided meditation you can follow if you want to meditate with your crystals:

1   Make sure you are in a quiet environment, away from loud noises, your phone, and other distractions.

2   You can decide to create a relaxing atmosphere by lighting an incense stick or using a subtle light.

3   Sit comfortably. If you sit in a cross-legged position, make sure your back is straight. You can hold your crystal in both hands or place it in front of you.

4   Look at your crystal: pay attention to its colors, texture, and shape.

5   Take three deep breaths and breathe gently after finishing. As you breathe let go of stress, anxiety, tension, and negative thought. Focus on your breath.

6   Now focus on your crystal: notice what you're feeling, the sensation you're exploring, and the vibration it is sending you.

7 When you feel like your contemplation is over, open your eyes. You can write down your feelings and repeat this session a second or third time. Remember to always cleanse yourself and your crystals. If you need to feel more grounded, use a smoky quartz, a boji stone, or another grounding crystal.

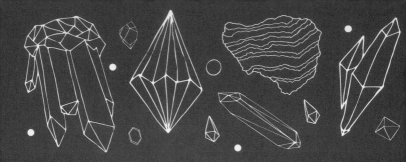

CHAPTER THREE:

FIFTY CRYSTAL PROFILES

In this chapter, we will discover the characteristics and spiritual properties of the fifty most common crystals, listed out in alphabetical order. I tried to include the ones that you are most likely to find in esoteric shops, in crystal healing therapies, and generally in the spiritual community.

Crystals come in all shapes, sizes, and colors. Many crystals are also known by different names, and the polishing and cutting process might drastically alter the appearances of their raw forms. However, the change of shape and the intervention of human hands won't change a crystal's powers and healing properties. Within this chapter, you will find all the spiritual, practical, and healing characteristics of each crystal and how you can use them in your daily life.

Always remember to treat your crystals respectfully, and keep in mind that spirit guides or beings who are there to help you during your spiritual journey dwell in many crystals. Knowing this, treat them as you would treat your dearest friend; use them as a bridge to connect with your highest self throughout your healing experience. You can use this guide to identify the right crystal for you by looking closely at their colors and aspects to find the one that most resonates with you and your needs.

Without further ado, I hope you will find your crystal companions and that their extraordinary powers will make your healing and spiritual journey magickal and beneficial.

AGATE

COLORS: black, blue, green, orange-red, pink, white

ORIGINS: United States, India, Morocco, Brazil, Mexico, Czech Republic, Botswana

CHAKRAS: Root chakra

ELEMENTS: earth

MAGICKAL ATTRIBUTES: use during difficult moments, protection for children from nightmares, personal growth, abundance, love, longevity, courage, protection

TIPS: Place it in your garden to foster plant growth; keep it in your pocket for protection.

Agate is formed by minuscule quartz laid down in bands. There are many different types of agate that come in different colors. All of them have the power to stabilize, ground, and center energies. When you have an agate near you, you might feel a sense of calm, peace, and harmony.

On a psychological level, agate can help improve your concentration, your logical thoughts, and self-acceptance. This powerful stone is also used to overcome traumas: it can help you get rid of negativity by creating a sense of safety and protection.

Spiritually, agate helps you develop awareness, mental stability, and confidence. Agate, when used for healing, can be placed on the stomach to stabilize the digestive system and to help with gastritis. Placing it on the heart will help cleanse our emotional sphere. It can also heal the eyes, uterus, lymphatic systems, and skin disorders.

AMAZONITE

COLORS: blue and green

ORIGINS: United States, Canada, Russia, Brazil, India, Mozambique, Austria

CHAKRAS: Heart and Throat chakras

ELEMENTS: earth and water

MAGICKAL ATTRIBUTES: inner truth, communication, success, calm

TIPS: Place near your bed to calm your mind before sleeping.

Amazonite is one of the most calming and soothing stones. It calms the nervous system, clears your mind from intrusive thoughts, and helps your brain process information. It is great for balancing feminine and masculine energies and experiencing universal love.

This stone is also used to protect us from cell phone radiation and electromagnetic pollution. Place amazonite between you and an electronic device or tape it to your phone to be protected. It is used to fight calcium deficiency and cavities, and is also beneficial in treating osteoporosis.

Spiritually, amazonite is great to open the Heart and Throat chakras for communication and also the Third Eye chakra for intuition.

AMBER

COLORS: deep orange, yellow, golden brown (when found green, it is artificially colored)

ORIGINS: Britain, Italy, Romania, Poland, Baltic Sea, United States, Russia, Germany

CHAKRAS: Sacral and Solar Plexus chakras

ELEMENTS: fire

MAGICKAL ATTRIBUTES: protection, success, love, money, connection with ancestors, purification

TIPS: Wear it during a ritual or a spell to increase your magickal powers. If you are a mom, wear it for some time and then pass it to your children. Do not cleanse it with salt.

Scientifically, amber is not considered a proper crystal, as it is formed by tree resins that solidify and become fossilized. That's why amber is also called "the trees' blood."

However, amber is very impressive in healing and cleansing our bodies. It has a strong connection to the Earth, which gives it a beautiful grounding power. It has the ability to transform negative energies into positive ones, and that's why we can use it to cleanse all seven of our chakras. Its warm energies help us find the motivation to achieve our dreams and bring stability into our life.

Other than bringing vitality, it is great for throat, stomach, kidneys, bladder, and liver treatments and for joint problems. We can place it on our wrists and throat (or on the specific areas that need the crystal's energy) to benefit from its incredible powers.

AMETHYST

COLORS: purple and lavender

ORIGINS: Argentina, United States, Canada, Britain, Brazil, Bolivia, Madagascar, Mexico, Uruguay, East Africa, Sri Lanka, Siberia

CHAKRAS: Third Eye and Crown chakras

ELEMENTS: air

MAGICKAL ATTRIBUTES: intuition, courage, calm mind, connection with spirits, breaking bad habits, balancing emotions, protection from negative energies

TIPS: Wear it as jewelry to benefit from it. Place an amethyst stone inside your pillow for a peaceful sleep. Do not leave it under the sun, to preserve its color.

Amethyst has extraordinary spiritual powers. It is used to protect from psychic attacks, transform negative energies, and enhance psychic abilities and powers. It is a natural tranquillizer that will help you deal with stressful situations and problematic environments.

When used properly, amethyst can have a calming and stimulating effect. For instance, holding an amethyst during a meditation session will help you concentrate deeply, abandoning the mundane world to gain great understanding of the universe. It can also stimulate your mind, encouraging you to make healthy decisions and set realistic goals. Traditionally, amethyst was worn to help overcome alcoholism and support sobriety and a healthy lifestyle. It is a great stone to combat anger, resentment, fear, rage, and anxiety.

This is why amethyst is considered one of the most powerful and resourceful crystals, as it not only helps our general health, but guides us on an introspective and spiritual journey to intuition, wisdom, love, and connection to the divine.

In a healing practice, we can use amethyst to cleanse our blood, relieve psychical and psychological pain, and fight headaches, migraines, and skin conditions. It can reduce bruises and help treat lung and respiratory diseases. It regulates our intestinal health and treats insomnia. I advise placing amethyst on your throat and heart to benefit from its qualities.

AQUAMARINE

COLORS: green and blue

ORIGINS: United States, Mexico, Russia, Brazil, Kenya, Pakistan, Zimbabwe, Ireland, Afghanistan

CHAKRAS: Throat chakra

ELEMENTS: water

MAGICKAL ATTRIBUTES: emotional clarity, peace, cleansing, protection when traveling over water, communication, empowerment, psychism, truth, courage

TIPS: Place it in a bottle of water and let it sit there for a while; take it out and drink the elixir to cleanse your body and aura. Do not leave aquamarine under the sun, as it might fade.

In ancient times, aquamarine was used to oppose dark entities and welcome benign spirits. This stone will bring peace into your life, calm your mind, and improve your courage and clarity. If you're a sensitive person, you might feel a strong connection with aquamarine, as it perceives hidden emotions and has a strong ability to understand how people feel.

It strengthens intuition and clairvoyance. It purifies the aura and the chakras, particularly the Throat chakra, enhancing your communication with the divine and aligning your physical and spiritual bodies. It is recommended you use aquamarine during meditation to increase your concentration and spiritual awareness.

Aquamarine can help heal sore throats, thyroid problems, and hay fevers, and it regulates hormones. It has a general tonic effect and it can be placed on specific body areas or over our eyes.

AVENTURINE

COLORS: light green, blue, red, yellow, brown, peach

ORIGINS: Italy, Brazil, Austria, China, Russia, India, Nepal, Tanzania

CHAKRAS: Heart chakra

ELEMENTS: earth

MAGICKAL ATTRIBUTES: awareness, empathy, communication, discernment, intellect, cure for broken hearts

TIPS: Use it to be protected from cell phone radiation.

Aventurine can have a pleasant, sparkly look caused by the sprinkles of other minerals it contains. It is a great stone to manifest prosperity, heal broken hearts, and get rid of emotional pain. It has the great power to reverse bad situations and to connect to the Devic Kingdom. The Devic Kingdom is where nature spirits live and is considered another dimension, as we cannot see it with our eyes. Some of the most popular spirits that are part of the Devic Kingdom are gnomes, elves, and fairies.

Aventurine brings empathy, compassion, and creativity, and also stabilizes our minds. It has the ability to lead whoever works with it to new life paths and enhance their sense of leadership. Aventurine is also very commonly used to protect us from environmental pollution and cell phone emanations.

Spiritually, it balances the feminine and masculine energies and also protects from vampiric attacks on the heart energies. It helps with our nervous system and connective tissue; it lowers cholesterol; and it helps with allergies, headaches, and migraines. It is also a great ally to heal the muscular system, lungs, heart, and skin problems.

BERYL

COLORS: blue, golden, yellow, green, white, pink

ORIGINS: United States, Russia, Australia, Brazil, France, Norway

CHAKRAS: Solar Plexus and Crown chakras

ELEMENTS: water

MAGICKAL ATTRIBUTES: optimism, wisdom, intuition, connection to spirits, purification

TIPS: Use it for scrying and to represent sea goddesses and gods.

Beryl is the apex of calming stones, perfect to help you through stressful days and overwhelming moments. It is an excellent guide to knowing what action is best, how to increase courage, and how to revive love in a marriage.

Beryl is great for practicing scrying and to use as a crystal ball; in the ancient past, it was also used to bring more rain. It is an excellent tool to heal our consciousness and create positive thoughts.

In a healing practice, we can use it to increase resistance to toxins and to treat the stomach, heart,

and liver. We can also create an elixir with water
and beryl to treat sore throats.

BLOODSTONE

COLORS: red-green

ORIGINS: Brazil,
China, Australia, India,
Czech Republic, Russia

CHAKRAS: Root chakra

ELEMENTS: earth

MAGICKAL ATTRIBUTES: purification, strength,
courage, vitality, altruism, grounding

TIPS: Place it in a bowl of water near your bed for
good sleep; wear it every day for good health.

Bloodstone was considered a very sacred and
powerful crystal in ancient times; it was believed it
was an oracle, giving guidance through sounds. It
is a great stone to increase creativity, dreaming, and
spirituality. In the magick realm, people believe it
can control the weather and provide the ability to
banish negative and evil spirits.

Bloodstone is also a potent revitalizer; it helps
you when you're mentally exhausted and in difficult

circumstances. It helps make you present in the moment and stay grounded in heart energy. You can use bloodstone to cleanse the lower chakras and reduce aggression and irritability.

As the name suggests, it is a wonderful tool to cleanse our blood, energy, liver, intestines, kidneys, and bladder. It stabilizes our blood circulation and it's helpful in healing acute infections. It is also advised you place it over the thymus as an immune stimulator.

CALCITE

COLORS: green, orange, clear, blue, pink, red, yellow, gray, brown

ORIGINS: United States, Britain, Brazil, Iceland, Belgium, Peru, Slovakia

CHAKRAS: all chakras, mainly used for the Crown chakra

ELEMENTS: fire and air

MAGICKAL ATTRIBUTES: purification, meditation, love, healing, prosperity

TIPS: Place it on your Third Eye during meditation

to increase your magickal powers; do not cleanse or leave in water or salt.

Calcite is a powerful ally for cleansing and amplifying all energies, based on your needs and intention. Having calcite in a room is an efficient cleansing method for getting rid of negative and stagnant energies.

It helps us connect to our higher self and increases our spiritual powers and psychic abilities. It is beneficial when you lose motivation, feel lazy, or are generally tired. Calcite is also great to elevate memory, insights, discernment, and calm in our minds.

Spiritually, you can use it during prayer or when contacting spirits. We can also use the different colors of calcite to cleanse all our chakras. Physically, it boosts calcium in our system, strengthening the joints and the skeleton; it is used in several medical supplements for this reason. It helps with our immune system and tissues. It is used for ulcers, skin conditions, and to support children's growth.

CARNELIAN

COLORS: red, orange, pink

ORIGINS: Brazil, United States, India, Uruguay, Peru, Czech Republic, Iceland, Romania

CHAKRAS: Sacral chakra

ELEMENTS: fire

MAGICKAL ATTRIBUTES: sensuality, passion, sex magick, motivation, confidence, success

TIPS: Keep it with you during the day to increase your motivation and to make others like you. Place it outside your door to welcome abundance and protection. Charge it under the sun.

Carnelian is highly connected to the sun, which gives it the attributes of passion, determination, and success. It is a stabilizing stone that grounds you, keeping you present in the moment. It brings vitality, creativity, positivity, and high energy. Carnelian improves self-belief, analytic abilities, and concentration in everyday life and during meditation.

In ancient times, carnelian was used to fight the fear of death, consecrating the importance of the cycle of life. You can use carnelian to cleanse all your crystals and bring love to your life, opposing the feelings of anger and resentment.

It is a powerful tool for fertility, as it stimulates the lower chakras; it strengthens our metabolism, combats rheumatism and arthritis, and helps with depression. Carnelian also helps to better absorb vitamins and minerals, improving the health of our organs and tissues.

CELESTITE

COLORS: blue, white, red, yellow

ORIGINS: Egypt, Britain, Peru, Madagascar, Mexico, Libya, Poland

CHAKRAS: Throat, Third Eye, and Crown chakras

ELEMENTS: air

MAGICKAL ATTRIBUTES: invocation of spirits, calm, prophetic dreams, harmony, opening the mind to the divine, confidence in your magickal powers, astral travel

TIPS: Use it for scrying or to increase the vibrations in a specific room. Do not leave it for too long under the sun and avoid contact with water.

Celestite is deeply related to magickal abilities and spiritual alignment. It helps you understand the universe and connect with all beings. It promotes enlightenment and stimulates clairvoyant communication. It develops purity, good fortune, and confidence in your powers; it brings balance, harmony, and truth, and it heals the aura.

Celestite is commonly used for astral travels—journeys out of the physical body. Artists use celestite to improve their creativity. It also calms tormenting emotions. It builds a great connection with infinite wisdom, inner peace, communication, and mental balance.

You can place celestite on your Third Eye to open connections with other energies and entities. It is also a wonderful healing crystal that relieves pain, eye problems, influenza, and muscular tensions.

CERUSSITE

COLORS: gray-black, white, yellow

ORIGINS: Namibia, France, Morocco, Italy, Scotland, Germany

CHAKRAS: Root and Crown chakra

ELEMENTS: earth

MAGICKAL ATTRIBUTES: creativity, hope, spiritual and energetic transformation, self-love, strength

TIPS: Make an elixir with water and cerussite and spray it in your room or onto plants to prevent pests and diseases; do not drink the water.

Cerussite is not only a beautiful, shiny stone, but an absolutely powerful crystal for bringing hope when you feel defeated, courage and self-belief when making decisions, and better communication skills in your personal and professional life. It is an excellent stone for grounding and making you feel connected to the Earth and at home wherever you are.

When cerussite forms a star shape, it is said that it helps create connections to extraterrestrials and reveals hidden secrets while meditating. It brings communication to spirits and our ancestors, sending us messages from them and showing us why we are on this planet, what our purpose is, and what path we should take. If you work in the creative field, cerussite might be a great stone to increase creativity, inventiveness, and spontaneity.

Cerussite has a few major health benefits. It is used to help people affected with Alzheimer's, dementia, Tourette's syndrome, and Parkinson's. It fights insomnia, nightmares, and obesity; it also improves muscles, bones, and involuntary movements and stimulates our brain, allowing us to process information more quickly.

CHALCEDONY

COLORS: white, blue, gray, pink, red

ORIGINS: United States, Austria, Brazil, Mexico, Czech Republic, Turkey, Iceland, Britain, Morocco, New Zealand, Slovakia

CHAKRAS: Sacral and Crown chakras

ELEMENTS: water

MAGICKAL ATTRIBUTES: prevention of nightmares, fear, curses, and psychic attacks; bringing protection, calm, kindness

TIPS: Place it near your bed to avoid nightmares; it also increases lactation. It is very common to find painted chalcedony—wet it to discover its true color.

Chalcedony is considered a very caring and nurturing stone that brings generosity, kindness, brotherhood, and harmony. It is a perfect crystal for healers and empaths, often used for telepathy and to absorb negative energies. It helps you develop good mental flexibility, communicative skills, and a positive mindset.

You can use chalcedony for a good cleansing and to improve the absorption of minerals into the body. It alleviates symptoms of dementia and heals the eyes, bones, spleen, and circulatory system.

CHRYSOPRASE

COLORS: apple green

ORIGINS: United States, Brazil, Australia, Russia, Poland, Tanzania

CHAKRAS: Heart and Sacral chakras

ELEMENTS: earth

MAGICKAL ATTRIBUTES: prosperity, abundance, healing, clairvoyance, fertility, meditation, tarot readings, healing broken hearts, hope, compassion, love

TIPS: Wear it to heal your inner child and release blocked emotions from your past.

Chrysoprase energizes our Heart and Sacral chakras, making us feel a universal sense of love and being highly channeled with the divine. It boosts our hope, compassion, and personal insights; it's a powerful tool to increase our meditative state and promote creativity and fidelity in business.

Chrysoprase is a calming stone, making us think of how our ego can affect our behavior and guiding us to improve ourselves and our mindset. It improves our sleep, protecting us from nightmares, and also stimulates our speech. This stone can encourage independence, but also commitment.

By being connected with our Sacral chakra, chrysoprase increases fertility and protects us from sexually transmitted illness. It softens mental illnesses, eye problems, gout, digestive problems, and hormonal imbalances. It heals claustrophobia and helps with the absorption of vitamin C. An elixir of chrysoprase and water can also help with stomach problems caused by stress.

CITRINE

COLORS: yellow, translucent yellow, brown

ORIGINS: United States, Brazil, Madagascar, Russia, France, Britain

CHAKRAS: Solar Plexus chakra

ELEMENTS: air

MAGICKAL ATTRIBUTES: manifesting, prosperity, success, creativity, courage, positive talk

TIPS: Amethyst can be heated to have a yellow color and be passed off as citrine. Fake citrine will be white at the bottom and dark yellow at the top, while real citrine will have a consistent yellow color. Its color might fade if left under the sunlight.

Citrine emanates the power of the sun through its radiant yellow color. It is a cleanser stone, able to regenerate our energies and all vibrations around us. It promotes prosperity, joy, abundance, and manifestation.

Citrine is probably one of the few stones that doesn't need a regular cleansing routine; because of its power to absorb and transform negative energies, it can be considered an auto-cleansing stone. Citrine has the ability to cleanse all seven of our chakras, and to activate the Solar Plexus and Crown chakras in particular. These qualities cause a major boost in intuition, protection, and alignment of our spiritual and physical bodies.

Apart from these beautiful powers, citrine is one of the main stones used to manifest abundance and prosperity. It is advised you place it in the left side corner of your house from the front door or the door of another individual room; this will increase the energy of your manifestation practice when manifesting money, success, and abundance.

On a psychological level, citrine increases self-belief, confidence, and creativity, and helps you be open to criticism. It transmits calm during stressful moments and gets rid of negative patterns, fear, and anger.

It's helpful to people affected with degenerative diseases, kidney and bladder infections, and eye problems. It soothes constipation and removes cellulite. A citrine elixir is advised to combat menopause symptoms and hormonal imbalances.

DANBURITE

COLORS: white, pink, yellow, lilac

ORIGINS: United States, Switzerland, Japan, Mexico, Czech Republic, Russia

CHAKRAS: Heart, Third Eye, and Crown chakras

ELEMENTS: air

MAGICKAL ATTRIBUTES: astral travels, cleansing, serenity, wisdom, spiritual transitions, patience, peace of mind

TIPS: Place it on your heart to amplify the Heart chakra's energy; place it inside your pillow for lucid dreams.

Danburite is no doubt a highly spiritual stone; it strongly activates your higher consciousness, channeling you to angelic realms. Working with this crystal tends to lead to eternal wisdom, karmic cleansing, and aura clarification.

We often see danburite in Buddhism, as its pure and bright light is found in the formation of a Buddha during the process of enlightenment. Danburite has very potent powers when it comes to activating the Heart, Third Eye, and Crown chakras, as well as opening up to higher dimensions.

It is used to clear allergies and fight chronic conditions and liver and gallbladder problems. You can also use it to relieve muscular pain and improve motor functions.

DIAMOND

COLORS: yellow, blue, brown, pink, clear white

ORIGINS: Australia, Brazil, India, Africa, United States

CHAKRAS: Crown chakra

ELEMENTS: air

MAGICKAL ATTRIBUTES: clarity, love, manifestation, abundance, wealth, creativity, the reduction of fear

TIPS: Wear against the skin or as an earring for manifesting and to be protected from cell phone emanations.

Diamond is one of the most expensive crystals, very rarely found in crystals or esoteric shops. Despite the high cost, it has amazing qualities such as promoting bonding in relationships, bringing love and cohesion into your life, and encouraging commitment and fidelity.

It's one of the rare crystals that don't need cleansing at all; it amplifies the energies of anything that comes into contact with it, very helpful when recharging other crystals. We have to be very intentional when working with a diamond, as it may increase positive but also negative energies.

It aids in enlightenment and connection to our higher minds. Diamond, moreover, brings clarity, creativity, and imagination; it fills the "holes" in your aura and reduces mental pain and fear. In a healing practice, it heals allergies, chronic diseases, and glaucoma.

EMERALD

COLORS: green

ORIGINS: Brazil, India, Austria, Tanzania, Egypt

CHAKRAS: Heart chakra

ELEMENTS: earth

MAGICKAL ATTRIBUTES: patience, calm, inspiration, love, balance, friendship, memory, psychic abilities

TIPS: Wear it on your little finger, ring finger, or right arm; do not wear it every day as it might bring negative feelings to light.

Emerald is known to be the stone of love, carrying within it loyalty and unconditional love; it is connected to our Heart chakra, stabilizing our feelings. It keeps balance in a relationship and strengthens friendships. It encourages us to take positive actions, maintain a balanced mind, and abandon negative emotions.

It is a great stone to increase our mental abilities and better our clairvoyant practice. Emerald will help us live a happy and positive life and get to know ourselves deeply. It brings wisdom and raises consciousness; we can also use it to heal influenza, lungs, muscles, eyes, the liver, and diabetes.

FLUORITE

COLORS: purple, green, blue, clear

ORIGINS: Brazil, Britain, United States, China, Peru, Norway, Germany, Canada, Australia

CHAKRAS: Throat and Third Eye chakras

ELEMENTS: water and air

MAGICKAL ATTRIBUTES: learning, communication with the fae, calm, productivity, protection from electromagnetic fields

TIPS: Hold it during meditation to increase your concentration. Keep it in your book to improve your learning. Do not leave it under sunlight or in water.

Fluorite is one of the New Age stones (crystals found during the New Age wave that began in the 1970s), with excellent properties like balance, mental focus, protection on a psychic level, cleansing of the aura, and the dispelling of negative energies. It provides stability, progress, truth, concentration, and coordination.

We can use fluorite to align our mind, body, and

spirit; we can use it to communicate with nature spirits, faeries, elves, and other fae folks. You can combine fluorite with other stones to increase their powers and efficiency.

It also aids in channeling the Akashic records for answers regarding your past lives. The Akashic records are a "library" that contains all past, present, and future information about every single one of us. Many people of different religions believe in them and some of them can "access" this information through powerful meditations.

Emotionally, this crystal is a very stabilizing one: it guides you to understand the impact of your emotions on your body. When practicing crystal healing, use fluorite to overcome infections, viruses, ulcers, and wounds. It helps strengthen bones, skin, teeth, cells, and bones. In addition, it is very powerful for healing rheumatism, sinusitis, general pain, blemishes, and wrinkles.

GARNET

COLORS: dark red, pink, orange, yellow, brown, black

ORIGINS: worldwide

CHAKRAS: Root and Heart chakras

ELEMENTS: fire

MAGICKAL ATTRIBUTES: love, commitment, energy, self-confidence, cleansing

TIPS: Use a garnet cube to bring success to your business. Wear it close to your heart to be sure of what partner to choose. Wear it to boost your energy during activities.

Garnet is a stone of love, passion, sensuality, health, and strength. It energizes and regenerates us whenever we work with it; it cleanses our chakras and purifies our energies. Red garnet especially controls kundalini energy and helps our sex sphere. Kundalini energy is the divine feminine energy that can be awakened by many kundalini practices. Once this energy is activated, it also activates all chakras and helps us reach enlightenment.

When we're going through uncertain periods, garnet will help us find a way to clear negative energies from our chakras. It helps your self-esteem and allows you to let go of what no longer serves you. It will stimulate your awareness and help you receive information about your past lives when in contact with your Third Eye. Not only does it open your heart, but it also helps you abandon taboos and embrace self-confidence.

Garnet is wonderful when it comes to regenerating

our metabolism, blood, heart, lungs, and DNA. It also helps assimilate vitamins and minerals. It is best worn on your finger, earlobes, or over the heart.

HEMATITE

COLORS: rust-red, red, silver

ORIGINS: Britain, Brazil, Italy, Switzerland, Canada

CHAKRAS: Root and Solar Plexus chakras

ELEMENTS: fire

MAGICKAL ATTRIBUTES: grounding, protection, harmony of mind and body, peace, self-esteem, confidence, concentration, memory

TIPS: Do not place it near inflammations. Do not wear it for a long period of time. Do not place it in water.

Hematite is very effective when it comes to grounding, protection against negative energies, and protection of our aura. It balances our mind, body, and spirit, and promotes self-confidence and expansion. It can help shy people become more extroverted and work past self-limitations.

Hematite is also useful in legal matters and for addictive personalities. It makes apparent all the needs that require fulfilment, boosting drive and passion for life. It enhances focus, concentration, and memory.

Physically, it helps heal blood conditions, kidney problems, legs, cramps, anxiety, and insomnia. It helps the absorption of iron and combats fever.

HOWLITE

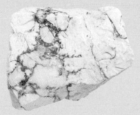

COLORS: white, green, blue (marbled appearance)

ORIGINS: United States

CHAKRAS: Root chakra

ELEMENTS: earth

MAGICKAL ATTRIBUTES: astral travels, calm, insomnia, wisdom, ambition, patience, absorbing negativity

TIPS: Keep it in your pocket to absorb negative energies. Keep it near your bed to fight insomnia. Howlite can touch water but not for a long period of time; you can also cleanse it in a bowl of brown rice.

Howlite is certainly a spiritual stone that connects you to other spiritual dimensions; it promotes astral travels and the receiving of wisdom. When placed on your Third Eye, it helps gather information about your past lives.

Howlite is also a very calming stone. It can help with insomnia and can calm overactive minds. It removes anger, selfishness, rage, and other disturbing feelings rooted in your past lives.

This crystal can help balance the calcium present in your bones, teeth, and soft tissues.

IRON PYRITE

COLORS: brown and gold

ORIGINS: United States, Britain, Canada, Italy, Chile, Peru

CHAKRAS: Solar Plexus chakra

ELEMENTS: earth

MAGICKAL ATTRIBUTES: patience, calm, inspiration, love, balance, friendship, memory, psychic abilities

TIPS: Use a cube of iron pyrite to manifest wealth.

Wear it in a pouch touching your throat for protection. Do not leave it in water.

Pyrite often resembles gold because of its bright and beautiful color; it is the stone of money, wealth, prosperity, and the material world. Placing pyrite on our desk during work can boost the energies that surround us, help us plan our professional life, and send us good ideas for our business. It fights anxiety, frustration, and the sense of inadequacy.

Pyrite can be utterly powerful when it comes to boosting self-confidence; that's why it has to be used cautiously if we want to avoid being too self-centered and aggressive, especially when used by men. It improves our memory, intuition, and creativity. It's helpful when we feel melancholic, particularly energy-drained, and when we need to protect our aura from energy leaks.

Iron pyrite is used to heal gastrointestinal problems that lead to insomnia, DNA damage, asthma, and bronchitis. It strengthens bones, our circulatory system, and cellular formations.

JADE

COLORS: green, orange, red, purple, white, blue, brown

ORIGINS: Middle East, Italy, United States, China, Russia, Myanmar

CHAKRAS: Heart chakra

ELEMENTS: water

MAGICKAL ATTRIBUTES: love, money, health, prosperity, generosity

TIPS: Use an animal-shaped coin or wear it on your left finger or arm to attract prosperity; wear it as a necklace touching your heart to increase sensitivity.

Jade is a sacred stone, especially in the Eastern world; it is now known internationally as a stone that brings prosperity, longevity, good luck, serenity, and wisdom. It protects whoever wears it, leaving open the doors to new friendships and good luck.

Jade has the power to calm the mind, removing negative thoughts and irritability. When we place it on our forehead we can expect dreams full of messages and prophecies. It encourages you to be who you really are, and become aware of your potential and knowledge.

Jade can cleanse kidneys and remove toxins; it aids in fertility and childbirth.

JASPER

COLORS: red, yellow, brown, black, blue, green, patterned

ORIGINS: worldwide

CHAKRAS: Root chakra

ELEMENTS: earth and fire

MAGICKAL ATTRIBUTES: tranquility, empathy, healing, protection, stability, grounding, cleansing

TIPS: Each differently-colored jasper crystal can be used to align the individual chakras based on their colors. Use it as a good luck charm. Place a big brown jasper in your room to absorb negative energies.

Jasper can be found in many different color shades with different types of properties; it is a stone of stability, safety, protection, and good health. It supports you during difficult moments and cleanses your chakras and aura. It is used during shamanic journeys and to balance yin and yang.

Jasper will help you feel grounded, stimulate your creativity, and aid you in making quick decisions.

Psychologically, jasper will encourage you to be honest with yourself and resolve any problem. You can use jasper during sex magick to prolong pleasure and regenerate your body. It heals the digestive and circulatory systems, as well as the sexual organs, and balances the minerals in your body.

JET

COLORS: black

ORIGINS: worldwide, mostly in the United States

CHAKRAS: Root and Crown chakras

ELEMENTS: earth

MAGICKAL ATTRIBUTES: banishing, binding, protection, removing negativity, stabilizing wealth

TIPS: Jet should be set in silver when worn as jewelry. Place jet over the heart to remove negativity; thereafter, wrap it with black cotton ribbon and bury it in the earth. Place it in the left corner of your house for wealth. Always cleanse it after each use.

Jet does look very much like charcoal; however, it is fossilized wood. It is also called "witch's amber," and in ancient times it was believed that jet would take part of the soul of whoever touched it.

Despite this belief, it has been used as a talisman since the Stone Age for its power to absorb negative energies and significantly reduce the feeling of fear. It is also said that whoever is attracted to this stone has had long permanency on Earth (having lived many previous lives).

Jet can be used during psychic practices, to stabilize our finances, and balance our moods. It helps fight depression, bringing stability and cleansing our Root chakra. It boosts the kundalini energy (see page 81), especially toward our Crown chakra. It helps treat migraines, menstrual cramps, colds, and stomach pain.

It is common to find black glass sold as jet, so always check its authenticity. Fake jet is very heavy and cold to the touch, while real jet is warm and light.

KUNZITE

COLORS: pink, lilac, clear, yellow, green

ORIGINS: United States, Brazil, Madagascar, Afghanistan

CHAKRAS: Heart chakra

ELEMENTS: earth

MAGICKAL ATTRIBUTES: unconditional love, meditation, protection from negativity, self-expression, intuition, introspection

TIPS: Place it on your Solar Plexus chakra to relieve panic. Wear it as a pendant or tape it onto electro-magnetic devices. It will fade if left under the sun.

Kunzite, when brought into your life, will motivate you to embrace self-expression, helping you to find a path without obstacles or pressure. It boosts introspection, intuition, and inspiration; it heals your heart from pains that come from your past lives and lifts your mood. Its high vibration will aid you in your healing journey, radiating unconditional love, humility, and communication.

Kunzite is also very effective when it comes to protection of people and the environment. Spiritually, it will free your aura from unwanted energies and remove attached entities and their influences. It stimulates your Heart chakra, aligning it with the Throat and Third Eye.

Kunzite heals the heart, the circulatory system, depression, and emotional stress. It boosts the immune system and can be used as an elixir to help with mental illnesses (the elixir cannot be drunk, as kunzite contains aluminum).

LABRADORITE

COLORS: black mixed with blue, yellow

ORIGINS: Canada, Italy, Australia, Madagascar, Finland, Scandinavia, Russia

CHAKRAS: Third Eye chakra

ELEMENTS: water and air

MAGICKAL ATTRIBUTES: growth, psychic abilities, protection, intuition, trust, calm, strength

TIPS: Have it near you to strengthen your magickal practice. Do not cleanse it in water, as it will dissolve.

Labradorite is the bringer of mysticism, magick, and occultism. It is a stone that will lead you to make universal connections, giving you the ability to travel to different worlds and past lives.

Labradorite is also a protective stone that will block any leakage from your aura. It sparks your intuition, psychic powers, and connection with your subconscious mind. It has a calming effect on overactive minds, and it revitalizes imagination and new ideas. Labradorite banishes insecurities and fear, especially negative feelings that are rooted in past lives. It boosts introspection, inner wisdom, and strength.

To work with labradorite, you can hold it near your Heart chakra while meditating or doing other rituals; when that's not possible, make sure it's near you to help you boost your power and your magick.

Labradorite heals colds, rheumatism, gout, and menstrual pain, regulates the metabolism, and balances the hormones.

LAPIS LAZULI

COLORS: blue and gold

ORIGINS: United States, Afghanistan, Chile, Italy, Egypt, Middle East

CHAKRAS: Throat and Third Eye chakras

ELEMENTS: water

MAGICKAL ATTRIBUTES: psychic abilities, connection to spirits, personal power, protection, protection from psychic attacks, reversing baneful magick, harmony, self-awareness, honesty, compassion, expression of love and feelings

TIPS: The best place to position it is between the sternum and the top of the head. It is very delicate and breaks easily; do not cleanse in water and salt.

Lapis lazuli is a beautiful blue stone with chips of pyrite that gives it a bright sparkle; it is a powerful, spiritual stone that will help you find your path and bring spiritual awareness. It opens the Third Eye and balances the Throat chakra, stimulating your spiritual journey. It enforces your connection with the spirit world, making it easier to find and communicate with spirit guides.

Lapis lazuli has the magnificent quality of recognizing psychic attacks and sending back harmful energies and curses. When there's an imbalance between the physical, mental, and spiritual bodies, the result could be depression, major anxiety, and lack of purpose. Lapis lazuli helps bring more balance between these aspects, promoting harmony and self-knowledge.

It helps you find the truth when you're seeking it, it amplifies your mental abilities, and it teaches you to express your feelings and listen. It is great to create a strong bond in friendships and romantic relationships and to increase creativity and clarity.

Lapis lazuli helps fight respiratory and thyroid problems, insomnia, and depression. It balances the immune system, alleviates hearing loss, lowers blood pressure, and cleanses our organs.

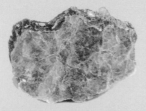

LEPIDOLITE

COLORS: purple and pink

ORIGINS: United States, Dominican Republic, Brazil, Madagascar, Czech Republic, Greenland

CHAKRAS: Throat, Third Eye, and Crown chakras

ELEMENTS: water

MAGICKAL ATTRIBUTES: cosmic awareness, prevention of anxiety and insomnia, mood stabilizing, independence, emotional healing, patience, happiness, lucid dreaming, self-expression, manifestation

TIPS: Place it between you and your laptop to absorb the emanations. Place it under your pillow for a peaceful sleep. Do not place it in water for extended periods of time.

Lepidolite is connected to the higher chakras; it opens and activates the Throat, Third Eye, and Crown chakras, removing any blockages. It is used during shamanic rituals and to gain access to Akashic Records (see page 80); it will help you understand the blockages from your past lives that are affecting your present, and it will advise you regarding what to do in the future.

Lepidolite dispels negativity and reduces the effects of depression, stress, obsessive thoughts, and dependency. It is helpful to overcome insomnia and disadvantageous behavior patterns. It contains lithium, which can be helpful to people with bipolar disorder and mood swings.

Lepidolite will aid you during hard transitions, encouraging you to never be dependent on someone else. It will guide you to make quick decisions and stay away from distractions; it will teach you to value your personal space and your healing journey.

Lepidolite has the power to alleviate any disease when placed in a specific body area. It helps heal allergies, strengthen the immune system, and alleviate Alzheimer's, epilepsy, menopause symptoms, sciatica, and joint problems.

MALACHITE

COLORS: green with dark bands and rings

ORIGINS: Romania, Russia, Zaire, the Democratic Republic of the Congo, Middle East

CHAKRAS: Heart chakra

ELEMENTS: earth

MAGICKAL ATTRIBUTES: life changes, grounding, protection, guard against negativity/strife in relationships, affinity with Devic forces (see page 62), scrying, growth

TIPS: Do not use it in elixirs, as it is highly toxic. Do not leave it in water and salt. Use it to absorb radiations of all kinds.

Malachite is a very powerful and intense stone that invites major life changes, new life paths, and drastic transformation. Despite its beauty and powers, it has to be handled with caution, and is best if used in the presence of a crystal therapist. This is because it's an extremely toxic stone that should be used only when polished.

If you'd like to make an elixir, malachite cannot touch the water. For this reason, you should place it near a bottle of water or spring water and let the power infuse from a distance. Avoid breathing its dust and do not use salt to cleanse it. You can use smoke or place it on a quartz cluster under the sun—before and after using it—instead.

Malachite amplifies both positive and negative energies; it is a grounding and healing stone with a deep connection to nature and Devic forces (see page 62). It cleanses and activates the chakras, helping you receive messages from your subconscious mind about the future. In fact, if placed on your Third Eye chakra, it will encourage psychic visions.

On a psychological level, malachite is a stone of big life changes. It brings transformations and promotes risk-taking and spiritual growth. You can use malachite to absorb negative energies, pollution, and radiation.

It helps with psychiatric illnesses, cramps, menstrual cramps, and sexual diseases. It assists during childbirth, lowers blood pressure, and alleviates asthma. It treats diabetes when worn around the wrist; however, it might cause high palpitations when in touch with the skin. If that occurs, take it off and wear rose quartz to bring calm.

MOLDAVITE

COLORS: dark green

ORIGINS: Germany, Czech Republic, Moldova

CHAKRAS: Crown chakra

ELEMENTS: fire

MAGICKAL ATTRIBUTES: extraterrestrial

connections, astral travels, spiritual growth, relieving homesickness, empathy, compassion

TIPS: Moldavite is a very fragile stone; be mindful when working with it. It can be in touch with water, but do not cleanse in salt.

Moldavite is part of the New Age stones (found in the 1970s), known to be an "extraterrestrial" crystal, formed when a meteorite hit the Earth. It is believed that moldavite is the result of the union between the extraterrestrial energies and Earth's energies. It is a very rare stone, mostly found in the Czech Republic near the river Moldau; that's why its existence on this planet is limited and it will eventually go extinct. It is also said that moldavite is on Earth to help the planet transition and heal, and that's why it often communicates messages regarding the ecology of the Earth.

It brings communication with higher beings, extraterrestrials, and Ascended Masters—beings that ended their cycle of reincarnation and operate from higher realms. When working with moldavite, it is useful to remember that its powers can make you feel off-balance and disconnected. To avoid these feelings, combine moldavite with boji stones (a variation of pyrite), clear quartz, hematite, and smoky quartz for grounding.

Its high vibrations clear your chakras, and when

in contact with your Third Eye it can give you the power to see the future and the past. Moldavite can also be very helpful for sensitive people who have always felt inadequate and not fully connected with this life on Earth, as it grounds and helps stabilize the physical and spiritual bodies.

It is a very unconventional crystal that can bring unexpected solutions, bring to light hidden memories, and, moreover, stabilize a strong connection to the Akashic Records (see page 80) and light body. The light body is often called the "astral body" and is our non-physical body. It is made of energy and allows us to "travel" to other dimensions.

Moldavite, in a healing practice, helps diagnose any illness, heal emotional traumas, and experience unconditional love.

MOONSTONE

COLORS: milky white, cream, yellow, blue, pink

ORIGINS: Brazil, Australia, India, Sri Lanka

CHAKRAS: Sacral, Solar Plexus, and Crown chakras

ELEMENTS: water

MAGICKAL ATTRIBUTES: long-lasting love, psychic powers, sensuality, new beginnings, intuition, empathy, emotional stability

TIPS: Pregnant women should always carry it with them. Some sellers might sell you opalite as "rainbow moonstone," but keep in mind that that won't have the same powers. Do not cleanse in salt.

Moonstone is frequently used because of its deep connection to the moon and moon goddesses. It brings intuition, calm emotions, empathy, and lucid dreams during the full moon. It is customary to use it for clairvoyance and to develop psychic abilities; it is also used in spells to manifest long-lasting love and to resolve misunderstandings.

Moonstone balances both female and male energies. It is particularly good for "alpha men" who want to discover their feminine side and for more aggressive women. It brings serendipity, emotional stability, and healing. When working with moonstone, always make sure that what you wish for doesn't turn into an illusion that takes you away from reality.

Moonstone was also traditionally used to prevent insomnia and sleepwalking. You can place it on your Solar Plexus chakra to understand deep, old emotions and then let go of them. Moonstone is particularly connected to the female reproductive cycle, healing menstrual diseases and regulating the biorhythmic clock. It helps the digestive system, water retention, skin and eye conditions, liver, and pancreas. It is great to promote fertility, pregnancy, childbirth, and breastfeeding.

NEBULA STONE

COLORS: black-green

ORIGINS: Mexico, United States (southwestern)

CHAKRAS: all chakras, especially Root and Crown chakras

ELEMENTS: all elements

MAGICKAL ATTRIBUTES: conscious awareness, manifesting, healing, memory recall

TIPS: Combine with moldavite to have powerful galactic connections. Place it in your bedroom for happy dreams. Wear it all the time to increase your energy and manifestations.

Nebula stone was discovered in 1995 in Mexico. As such, it is a fairly new stone and its powers are still yet to be fully discovered. It has a beautiful, nebula-like formation in a dark green background. The lighter parts are formed by the presence of quartz, which amplifies the energies of the other minerals present in the nebula stone.

Quartz makes nebula stone very easy to program; that's why it is a very powerful ally for manifesting. The riebeckite present in the stone will enhance your psychic abilities; the aegirine will stimulate kundalini energies and clear your aura; the anorthoclase will help you during your transformation journey.

It connects you with the light energies and with the cosmos and all beings. Light energy is a type of energy we can activate within; it is highly vibrational, expansive, positive, and full of love.

Quartz will help you feel grounded, expanding your understanding of why you exist and increasing your vitality. Nebula stone is great to get rid of toxins present in your body and stimulate cell growth and cell renewal.

OBSIDIAN

COLORS: black, blue, brown, gold-sheen, dark red, green, silver

ORIGINS: worldwide

CHAKRAS: Root chakra

ELEMENTS: earth and fire

MAGICKAL ATTRIBUTES: divination, scrying, protection, truth, healing, protection against psychic attacks, elimination of blockages

TIPS: Run under water to cleanse it every time you use it. Get an athame made of obsidian to perform powerful spells. Use it as a mirror for scrying.

Obsidian is formed when molten lava meets cold water or air and solidifies. Its formation is a result of the combination of destruction and creation, of fire and ice. It is a limitless stone that always goes to the core of the matter.

It works extremely fast and brings to light any hidden truth or blockages. That's why it is advised you use it with a crystal therapist, as it may upset us or bring too many negative emotions at once. It is a stone used by therapists because it helps release emotions and deeply understand the root of problems.

Obsidian will protect you from all negative energies, helping your Root chakra ground you to Earth; it guides you to past lives to understand old traumas and improve your present life. Because of its nature, placing obsidian near you could agitate you, and could either make you feel stressed or calm you.

It encourages you to practice shadow work, grow on all levels, and discover the unknown. Shadow work is a practice that encourages us to face the darkest emotions in our subconscious (this could be traumas, patterns, or behaviors), which we try to hide from ourselves. This eventually leads to personal and spiritual growth. Obsidian aids you in exploring who you really are, finding your identity, and amplifying compassion. It detoxifies our body, soothes digestive problems, and reduces arthritis, joint pain, injuries, and cramps.

ONYX

COLORS: black

ORIGINS: Italy, Brazil, India, United States, South Africa, Mexico, Russia

CHAKRAS: Root chakra

ELEMENTS: earth

MAGICKAL ATTRIBUTES: protection, self-power, reversing curses, strength, healing, self-control

TIPS: It is advised you wear it on the left side of your body. It holds all the memories of those who carry it, so be careful about who can hold it. Carry it with you when you're in a group of people with ill intentions or negative energies.

Onyx facilitates the connection with the divine and higher self. It helps you navigate difficult times and stressful events. It boosts your personal power, and will give you the ability to find solutions in stressful circumstances. It can allow you to see the future and it is commonly used in spells for protection against dangerous situations and to reverse curses.

It stimulates self-confidence, balances yin and yang, and its capacity to hold memories helps you connect to past lives. It promotes the duality within ourselves, calms overwhelming feelings, and guides us to wise decisions.

It was traditionally believed that onyx held demonic forces, and yet some use it for protection in the modern day. Meditate holding it, and pay attention to what your feelings are. Onyx can also heal bones, feet, teeth, and blood problems.

OPAL

COLORS: white, yellow, orange, blue, purple, pink, red, green, black, brown

ORIGINS: Mexico, Australia, Peru, Canada, Brazil, Britain, Honduras, United States

CHAKRAS: Solar Plexus and Heart chakras

ELEMENTS: water

MAGICKAL ATTRIBUTES: increase magickal powers during a spell, inner beauty, psychic visions, love, desire, passion, loyalty, connection to past lives

TIPS: When worn it has the power to make you go unnoticed by others. Do not cleanse with salt, and be aware that sunlight will fade its colors. Cleanse it with other crystals, moonlight, or smoke.

Opal has many different qualities because of the variations in its colors; it vibrates very lightly and stimulates our cosmic consciousness. It has always been associated with love and passion, enhancing desire.

It boosts positive emotions and promotes loyalty and spontaneity. It has the unique power to absorb energy, amplify it, and send it back to its source. It supports strong powers such as psychic and mystical visions. Opal boosts self-worth and one's potential. It stabilizes emotions and teaches you the rule of karma: what you put out into the world is what you will eventually receive.

In the healing field, opal treats fevers, infections, eye problems, and Parkinson's.

PERIDOT

COLORS: honey, olive green, red, brown

ORIGINS: Ireland, Brazil, United States, Sri Lanka, Canary Islands, Egypt, Russia

CHAKRAS: Solar Plexus and Heart chakras

ELEMENTS: earth

MAGICKAL ATTRIBUTES: protection of the aura, cleansing, clearing blockages, forgiveness, the elimination of jealousy, anger, and lethargy

TIPS: Wear it in contact with the throat or liver.

Peridot cleanses, opens, and activates the Heart and Solar Plexus chakras. It releases old emotions that no longer serve us. It protects our aura and purifies our astral and physical bodies. It is good for supporting people with bipolar disorders and fights hypochondria.

Peridot gets rid of old and negative patterns, helping us understand our destiny and purpose. It strengthens our level of awareness and helps us take responsibility for our mistakes and move on. It promotes spiritual truth and resolves hard problems in relationships.

Peridot tones up our body and reinforces our metabolism, heart, thymus, intestines, and skin. It is also used to alleviate the pain during childbirth if placed on the chest and belly.

QUARTZ

COLORS: clear, blue, pink, purple, green, orange, gray

ORIGINS: worldwide

CHAKRAS: Crown chakra

ELEMENTS: fire

MAGICKAL ATTRIBUTES: clearing, cleansing, healing, amplification, memory, psychic abilities

TIPS: Place any crystal near clear quartz to amplify its energies. Use a quartz point to strengthen any object's energy. Use it to harmonize all chakras.

Quartz is one of the most common crystals in the world. It has great healing energy and amplifies intentions. Its extraordinary powers heal whoever holds it, as it knows exactly where we have blockages and where specifically we need help. It contains all colors, which gives it a universal power. It holds and stores memories and information and dissolves karmic seeds (the dormant essence of karma).

It fortifies psychic abilities and reinforces concentration during meditation. It has the ability to absorb, store, regulate, realize, and unblock energy. It is quickly programmable, cleanses our soul and spiritual body, and balances our physical one. Quartz is an optimal energy saver; for instance, you can attach it to a fuel line in your car to reduce fuel consumption (though this should not be attempted without the help of an experienced mechanic).

It is very effective when it comes to healing any disease and condition. It cleanses our organs, stimulates our immune system, and raises the efficiency of acupuncture by 10%.

RHODOCHROSITE

COLORS: pink and orange

ORIGINS: United States, South Africa, Argentina, Uruguay, Russia

CHAKRAS: Heart and Solar Plexus chakras

ELEMENTS: water and fire

MAGICKAL ATTRIBUTES: generosity, inner peace, compassion, friendship, creativity, happiness, relaxation, self-discovery, self-awareness

TIPS: Place it on the higher part of the spine to help with migraines. Avoid contact with water.

Rhodochrosite is one of the most powerful stones to bring self-love into one's life. It is commonly used to help heal after sexual abuse. It helps open your heart and attract real love, and even if sometimes it might not be pleasant, it teaches us many life lessons.

It instructs you to not be in denial when experiencing traumatic events and deeply difficult emotions. It gently brings painful feelings to light, giving you the opportunity to deal with them and release them. It promotes truth, positive behaviors, and expression of feelings.

Rhodochrosite will help you get through depression, guiding you in your healing journey and welcoming light into your existence. It will symbolize everything you don't want to face, acting as the carrier of truth and authenticity. It removes paranoia and irrational thoughts, improving self-worth and freedom of being.

Rhodochrosite will alleviate asthma, respiratory problems, kidney problems, and unstable blood pressure. Its elixir relieves skin conditions and infections and balances the thyroid.

ROSE QUARTZ

COLORS: pink

ORIGINS: South Africa, United States, Brazil, Japan, India, Madagascar

CHAKRAS: Heart chakra

ELEMENTS: earth

MAGICKAL ATTRIBUTES: unconditional love, meditation, protection from negativity, self-expression, intuition, introspection

TIPS: Wear it over the heart to attract love and romance; make rose quartz elixirs for self-love and to attract and receive love.

Rose quartz is representative of unconditional love and peace. It is the Heart chakra's crystal, purifying and opening our hearts. It brings inner peace, self-love, true love, and harmony. It reassures you when you need it and helps you through crises. It works very gently on whoever uses it, transforming negative feelings into love.

It is advised you hold rose quartz while meditating to reinforce positive affirmations and intentions and to appreciate all kinds of beauty. It heals broken hearts and releases emotions that no longer serve us. Rose quartz opens your heart, allowing you to love yourself and receive and give love.

You can place rose quartz near your bed or on the right corner of your house, the farthest from the entrance or door. It will spark the love in your relationship, restoring harmony, complicity, and trust. Its power is so strong that sometimes the presence of amethyst is needed to calm its effects.

Rose quartz is great for healing our physical heart, chest and lung problems, kidneys, the circulatory system, Alzheimer's, Parkinson's, and dementia.

RUBY

COLORS: red

ORIGINS: Madagascar, India, Sri Lanka, Cambodia, Kenya, Russia

CHAKRAS: Root and Sacral chakras

ELEMENTS: fire

MAGICKAL ATTRIBUTES: zest for life, passion, confidence, courage, laughter, motivation, protection from psychic attacks and vampirism, positive dreams, wealth, abundance

TIPS: Use it to spark your sex life and when performing money magick. Wear it on any finger, over the heart, and on the ankle.

Ruby is the crystal of passion for life, motivation, abundance, and wealth. It balances our energy; however, if you're a sensitive person, it might overstimulate you. It revitalizes the Heart chakra and your physical heart. It is a great talisman for protection from vampires and psychic attacks.

It encourages you to get rid of all negative energies, bringing positivity, concentration, and help setting realistic goals. It encourages you to be strong during adverse times, helps you to overcome laziness, and calms hyperactive behaviors.

Ruby cleanses our body, blood, heart, and circulatory system. It heals the lymph nodes, fevers, kidneys, and reproductive organs.

SELENITE

COLORS: deep white, green, brown, blue, orange

ORIGINS: Britain, France, Mexico, United States, Germany, Austria, Greece, Poland, Russia

CHAKRAS: Crown chakra

ELEMENTS: air

MAGICKAL ATTRIBUTES: clarity, intuition, transformation, peace, awareness, connection to spirits, meditation, cleansing, charging, dissolving negative energies, angelic connection

TIPS: Use a selenite wand to dissolve any negative and unwanted energies and vibrations by moving it over your entire body several times. Selenite is very delicate and should not be put in contact with water and salt. It cleanses and charges all crystals.

Selenite's name comes from the name Selene. Selene is a Greek goddess connected to the moon. Selenite is a calming stone that gives you peace and a deep connection to higher and angelic realms. It enhances telepathy, peace in the house, and insight.

Selenite, with its translucent color, has ethereal qualities, emanating pure vibrations and reaching all beings. It is considered one of the most powerful crystals on Earth. It has outstanding effects during meditation and links you to the light body (see page 99). You can place a big piece of selenite in your house to ensure peace and protection.

A wand of selenite can also be used to detach any entities from your body and dissolve unwanted vibrations. You can use selenite for scrying in order to see the future, your past lives, and the best solutions to your current problems.

Selenite is helpful to combat epilepsy, reinforce flexibility, and aid in breastfeeding.

SERPENTINE

COLORS: green, dark green, brown, red, yellow, white

ORIGINS: Cornwall (UK), Norway, Italy, United States, Russia, Zimbabwe, Greece

CHAKRAS: Heart chakra

ELEMENTS: earth

MAGICKAL ATTRIBUTES: protection, protection against evil energies and curses, meditation, connection to past lives, control over life, wisdom, longevity, wealth, new relationships

TIPS: Use serpentine to clear all chakras. Wear three jewelry pieces made of serpentine: one for protection, one for new relationships, and one for wealth. You can make elixirs with serpentine, but be careful to avoid using chrysotile serpentine, as it is highly toxic.

Serpentine is deeply related to kundalini energy, which is sometimes compared to a snake, as it is the life energy that flows in our body. The word "serpentine" comes from the Latin *serpentines,* which means "belonging to a snake."

It supports wisdom, meditation, and healing; it helps you understand the faces of spirituality and balances mental instabilities, helping you feel more in control of your life. It activates the Crown chakra, stimulating intuition and psychic abilities.

Serpentine is great for protection and starting new relationships, as it will keep away people who don't align with your personality. It is also great to promote peace in a house.

Use serpentine to help manage diabetes, to improve the absorption of magnesium and calcium, and to eliminate parasites.

SODALITE

COLORS: blue

ORIGINS: France, Brazil, Greenland, Russia, North America, Romania

CHAKRAS: Throat and Third Eye chakra

ELEMENTS: air and water

MAGICKAL ATTRIBUTES: unconditional love, meditation, protection from negativity, self-expression, intuition, introspection

TIPS: Place it in every room of your house to harmonize it. Use it to absorb electromagnetic waves. Do not cleanse in water or salt.

Sodalite is the artist's stone, known for increasing creativity and inspiration while also protecting the musician, painter, or sculpture's ideas from being stolen. It combines intuition with intellect, delivering information from the higher realms.

This crystal brings inner peace in addition to calming hot-tempered personalities. It is a stone of truth, encouraging those who wear it to always follow their beliefs. It promotes communication, solving misunderstandings and divergences between people.

Sodalite is great when used by groups of people as it brings creative ideas, companionship, and solidarity. It reinforces rational thoughts, removing mental confusion and rigid mindsets. It will dissolve fear, guilt, and phobias and help overcome panic attacks. Sodalite can be used for shadow work, as it will bring the sides of your personality you don't want to face to light without judgment.

It is helpful when the metabolism needs balance, when there is a calcium deficiency, and when you need to boost the immune system. It heals fevers, insomnia, vocal cords, and digestive disorders.

SUNSTONE

COLORS: yellow, orange, brown

ORIGINS: United States, Norway, Canada, Greece, India

CHAKRAS: Sacral and Solar Plexus chakras

ELEMENTS: fire

MAGICKAL ATTRIBUTES: joy, strength, courage, optimism, self-love, empowerment, cleansing, abundance, sexual energy

TIPS: Use it for cord-cutting spells and attraction spells. Benefit from its powers under the sun.

Sunstone, as the name suggests, is connected to the sun and holds all its powers, such as winning energies and attitude, positivity, determination, empowerment, and joy. You can use it to cleanse all chakras and bring your inner light to the surface. It has the power to connect to the light, and it regenerates you during meditations, especially under the sun. Sometimes it contains freckles of hematite, which makes it a good crystal for manifestation.

Sunstone is great for removing energies and people that hold you back: you can place a piece of sunstone over the photo of who or what is restraining your freedom, and this will set you free from any unwanted influences.

Keep sunstone with you in your everyday life if you're struggling with saying "no" or if you're in a codependent relationship with a family member, friend, or partner. It is also used as an antidepressant, during seasonal changes of mood, or for protection against discrimination. When placed on your Solar Plexus chakra, it will remove repressed feelings.

It is great to balance the nervous system, organs, and cartilage problems. It helps heal general pain and chronic pains, especially those related to the throat and ulcers.

TIGER'S EYE

COLORS: gold, brown, red, blue, pink

ORIGINS: South Africa, Mexico, United States, Australia, India

CHAKRAS: Sacral, Solar Plexus, and Third Eye chakras

ELEMENTS: earth and fire

MAGICKAL ATTRIBUTES: legal matters, protection, protection against curses, truth, integrity, psychic abilities, manifesting, self-worth, lifting moods

TIPS: Carry it with you when you wish to identify a liar. Use it in spells for legal matters. Do not wear it for a long period of time, as its effects might be overwhelming.

Tiger's eye is a very protective stone that carries the power of the Earth and the sun, which makes it very versatile. It is a stone of integrity, .pride, clarity, intention, and justice. It stimulates the lower chakras, raising the kundalini energy (see page 81).

You can place it on your Solar Plexus chakra to increase confidence, on your throat to speak your truth, and on your Third Eye to boost your psychic abilities. It helps people who struggle to commit. It is excellent for grounding and empowering your manifestation practice.

Tiger's eye will show you not only your needs, but what other people need, as well as what they desire. It differentiates between what you want and what you need, resolving difficulties and promoting self-criticism and self-worth. It alleviates mental illnesses and personality disorders and it supports the healing of those with addictive personalities.

Tiger's eye helps the healing process in reproductive organs, broken bones, and eye problems.

TOPAZ

COLORS: clear, blue, orange-yellow, red, pink, green, brown

ORIGINS: United States, Sri Lanka, Pakistan, Mexico, India, Australia, South Africa

CHAKRAS: Solar Plexus, Third Eye, and Crown chakras

ELEMENTS: air (and also earth and fire)

MAGICKAL ATTRIBUTES: empathy, forgiveness, truth, clarity, love, good fortune, health, abundance, confidence, inner wisdom, expression, meditation

TIPS: Wear it on your ring finger. Use an elixir made with topaz on your skin. Place it in the relationship corner of the house (far right) to improve and strengthen your romantic relationship.

Topaz is a caring and understanding stone. It's able to direct its energy where it is needed, promoting truth, wisdom, and love. It brings body, mind, and soul into union and aids in clear communication. It has both positive and negative energies which help you channel your desires and manifest them into reality.

Topaz attracts joy, good health, generosity, and success, and it clears the aura. It leads you to feel confident, engage in self-realization, and spreads positive energies. It helps you solve problems, become self-aware, and express your ideas.

Topaz can help fight anorexia and weak nerves and promotes good health.

TOURMALINE

COLORS: black, pink, purple, red, yellow, blue-green, brown, blue, watermelon

ORIGINS: United States, Madagascar, Nigeria, Sri Lanka, Brazil, Italy, Africa, Namibia, Tanzania, Australia, Afghanistan

CHAKRAS: Root and Throat chakras

ELEMENTS: earth

MAGICKAL ATTRIBUTES: protection, protection for sensitive people, peace, good sleep, cleansing, purifying, garden magick, growth, self-confidence, release of tension

TIPS: Place it near the window to keep away negativity. Avoid contact with water.

Tourmaline is a very powerful stone for protection; it protects you from negative energies, during spells and rituals, and creates a protective shield around the body. It has a great connection with the Devic forces (see page 62) and it can be used for scrying and finding the right direction to take in specific situations. It grounds your spiritual body, clearing and balancing all seven chakras; a tourmaline wand can clear your aura from negative energies and dissolve blockages.

Tourmaline is also a great tool in garden magick. It is a natural insecticide, so it keeps the pests away and helps your garden and plants grow healthily.

Mentally, tourmaline guides you to discover who you really are, boosting self-confidence, inspiration, and compassion, while getting rid of fear and paranoia. It balances female and male energies. It heals your mind, turning negative thoughts into positive patterns.

Tourmaline comes in many different colors. To understand which one best suits you, meditate with them and observe what you feel with each one. For instance, yellow, red, and brown tourmaline revitalize your sexual energy, while blue tourmaline activates your Throat and Third Eye chakras, connecting you to spiritual freedom and self-expression.

Tourmaline can be used to treat dyslexia, debilitating diseases, and arthritis, and reinforces the immune system.

TURQUOISE

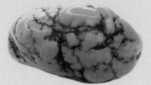

COLORS: turquoise, green, blue

ORIGINS: United States, Mexico, China, France, Egypt, Peru, Arabia, Iran, Afghanistan, Poland, Russia

CHAKRAS: Throat and Third Eye chakras

ELEMENTS: air and fire

MAGICKAL ATTRIBUTES: cleansing, purifying, environmental awareness, protection, communication, intuition, meditation, expression, self-realization, creativity, inner calm

TIPS: When overloaded, turquoise might break into pieces. Place it anywhere you feel pain. Wear a turquoise ring when performing healing spells. Sometimes you might find howlite sold as turquoise or turquoise that has been artificially painted. Do not cleanse turquoise in water, salt, or sunlight; it is best if cleansed with smoke or under the moonlight.

Turquoise is a healing stone par excellence; it brings balance to both the spiritual and physical body. For thousands of years, it has been used as a healer and protector. In ancient times, it was believed to change color to warn people of negativity, risks, and danger.

Turquoise absorbs the energy and vibrations of whoever touches it, removing any negative energy. It can strengthen your bond with the Earth, bringing awareness to ecology and the general state of the planet. It boosts communication with the physical world as well as the spiritual one.

Turquoise absorbs electromagnetic pollution, balances the chakras, and helps you gets rid of self-sabotaging behaviors. It stabilizes mood changes and stimulates inner peace and romantic relationships. It is a great stone to combat fatigue, depression, and panic attacks.

100 SUPPLEMENTARY CRYSTALS

AGATE (BLACK): protection, winning competitions, protection of material objects from being stolen

AGATE (BLUE): self-acceptance, expression of feelings, removal of anger, activation of the Throat chakra (tip: you might find artificially-made glass sold as blue agate)

AGATE (FIRE): calm, protection, returning harm sent from people, vitality, sexual energy, introspection, fighting addiction

AGATE (MOSS): connection to nature, beneficial to people employed in botany or agriculture, new beginnings, wealth, abundance, self-expression, aid in healing depression

AMETRINE: promotes astral travels and protects during them, meditation, protection against psychic attacks, opens the Third Eye, concentration, optimism

ANGELITE: awareness, peace, connection to angelic realms, healing, protection for the environment, self-protection, self-expression, compassion, telepathy, astrology

APATITE: manifesting, communication, self-expression, humanitarian attitude, extroversion, teamwork, reduction of irritability, anger, and frustration

ARGONITE: grounding, encouragement to take care of the Earth, patience, acceptance, discipline, flexibility, tolerance, self-acceptance, calm

ATACAMITE: opening the Third Eye, spiritual visions, clarity, meditation, astral travels, unconditional love

AZURITE: psychic powers, enlightenment, astral travels, meditation, communication, memory, stimulating the Third Eye, welcoming the unknown, calming extroverted people, encouraging introverted people to open up

BERYL (GOLDEN): scrying, magickal rituals, purity of being, manifesting, opening Solar Plexus and Crown chakras

BERYL (PINK/MORGANITE): enjoying life, love, loving behaviors, calm, leading one to see unexpressed feelings, cleansing and activating the Heart chakra

BERYL (CHRYSOBERYL): compassion, forgiveness, new beginnings, creativity, self-worth,

opening the Crown chakra

BERYL (CHEYSOBERYL: CAT'S EYE): grounding, intuition, removing negative energies from the aura, protection, confidence, happiness, good luck, increase in attractiveness

BOJI STONE: grounding, protection, helping overcome blockages, shadow work (tip: you'll need two to balance the energies: the round and smooth ones have female energy, and the angled ones have male energy)

BRONZITE: mindfulness, meditation, sending back curses, amplifying energy

CALCITE (BLACK): past lives' regression, bringing old memories to light

CALCITE (BLUE): relaxation, fighting anxiety, communication, clearing energies and sending them back to the sender

CALCITE (CLEAR): cleansing and aligning all chakras, healing souls (tip: when it has a rainbow it brings big changes)

CALCITE (GREEN): balancing the mind, removing rigid beliefs, absorbing negativity, communication

CALCITE (PINK): connection to angelic realms, unconditional love, forgiveness, relief from anxiety, helping people with traumas and those who have experienced assault

CHALCEDONY (RED): strength, persistence, manifesting

CHIASTOLITE: protection, protection against curses, harmony, problem-solving, helping in transition after death, dissolving illusions, stabilizing emotions

CHLORITE: bringing positivity into the environmental energy field, protecting against psychic attacks and negative entities

CHRYSANTHEMUM STONE: spiritual strength, harmony, good luck, self-growth, love

CHRYSOCOLLA: discretion, wisdom, meditation, communication, impermanence, cleansing and boosting all chakras

DALMATIAN STONE: mental freedom, warning you before dangerous situations, dissolving obsessive thoughts

DESERT ROSE: powerful connection between physical and astral realms

DIOPTASE: mindfulness, recalling past lives' memories, inner child, emotional healing, dissolving sorrow, helping you identify who is holding you back

EPIDOTE: releasing resentment and the victim mindset, shadow work

FLUORITE (BLUE): creativity, communication, calming or boosting energies, spiritual awakening

FLUORITE (CLEAR): connection to spirits, great for beginners, getting rid of dark thoughts, protection against psychic attacks, aligning all chakras, stimulating the Crown chakra, energizing the aura

FLUORITE (GREEN): prosperity, business strategies, success in business, growth, dissolving emotional traumas, absorbing negative energies in the environment, cleansing the aura, all chakras, and the mind

FLUORITE (PURPLE): meditation, psychic abilities, good in tarots or oracles' readings, stimulates the Third Eye chakra

FLUORITE (YELLOW): creativity, group activities, teamwork

FLUORITE (YTTRIAN): wealth, abundance, manifesting, mental activities

FUCHSITE: helping to learn herbal and holistic treatments, well-being, helping you to accompany someone's path without overwhelming yourself, overcoming codependency and emotional blackmail, resilience after traumas

GIRASOL: help during big changes, focus, prevention from feeling overwhelmed

HAG STONE: A hag stone is any stone with a natural hole; you can wear it daily. It brings good luck, connection to the faeries' realm, prosperity, and protection.

ICELAND SPAR: providing hidden information, showing you hidden and secret messages behind symbols, words, or conversations

IDOCRASE: freedom, connection to the higher self, healing from past lives' traumas, security, clarity, creativity

IOLITE: overcoming bad habits, fighting addictions, inner strength, activating the Third Eye, self-expression, balancing our aura, releasing codependency, helping to solve problems in relationships

JADE (BLUE): reflection, serenity, peace, dissolving overwhelming feelings

JADE (BROWN): comfort, grounding, help in adapting to new environments

JADE (GREEN): passion, peace in relationships, calm

JADE (LAVENDER): healing emotional traumas and pain, inner peace, encouragement to set boundaries

JADE (RED): passion, love, releasing anger and tension

JADE (WHITE): decision-making, getting rid of distractions

JASPER (BASANITE): scrying, prophetic dreams, spiritual visions, connection to the higher consciousness

JASPER (BLUE): balances yin and yang, stabilizing the aura, astral travels, stimulating the Throat chakra, positivity

JASPER (BROWN): connection to Earth, stability, ecological awareness, meditation, regression to past lives, astral travels

JASPER (GREEN): balance, health, stimulation of the Heart chakra, healing obsessions, toxic relationships, and negative patterns

JASPER (MOOKAITE): calm, desire for new adventures, versatility, decision-making, new perspectives

JASPER (PICTURE): representation of Mother Earth, containing messages from the past, showing hidden and repressed feelings, comfort, harmony

JASPER (RED): stimulating, grounding, balance, calm, dream recall, stimulating the Root chakra, assistance in the rebirthing transition, bringing of slow changes

JASPER (YELLOW): protection during astral travels and spiritual practices, stimulating the Solar Plexus chakra, self-confidence, problem-solving, calm

KUNZITE (LILAC): symbolization of infinity, help in the transition after death, help to reach enlightenment

KUNZITE (YELLOW): protecting the aura from radiations, aligning all chakras

KYANITE: meditation, psychic abilities, connection to spirit guides, connection to higher beings, aligning all chakras and our aura, stabilizing the aura, banishing unwanted energies, removing blockages, illusion, anger, stress, and frustration

LABRADORITE (YELLOW): clairvoyance, channeling to higher realms and beings, access to the highest level of consciousness, higher wisdom, energizing the Solar Plexus chakra

LARIMAR: attracting good people into your life, love, peace, tranquility, control over your life, constructive thoughts, connection to your inner child

LAVA ROCK: storing energies until you need to use them, absorbing negative energies

MAGNETITE: grounding, temporarily aligning the chakras and our etheric bodies, connection to the Earth, love, loyalty, commitment, tenacity, removing attachment, fear, anger, and grief, containing both positive and negative energies, use in banishing and attracting spells

MERLINITE: attracting magickal and mystical energies, holding the knowledge of shamans, alchemists, and other workers of magic, delivering your messages to spirits to manifest your desires

MOTHER-OF-PEARL: calming energies, problem-solving, dissolving anger and aggression

OKENITE: connection to the higher self, help finding your purpose, help to grow as a person, karmic healing, truth, self-forgiveness, releasing old patterns

OPAL (BLUE): connection to the Throat chakra, healing past lives' blockages

OPAL (BROWN): connection to the Sacral chakra and reproductive organs, releasing sexual tensions

OPAL (CHERRY): cleansing and activating the Root and Sacral chakras, clairvoyance, help feeling centered

OPAL (FIRE): personal power, protection, good business, energy amplifying, justice, help letting go of the past

OPAL (GREEN): cleansing, emotional healing, improving relationships, stabilizing the mood, meditation, connection to the Root and Crown chakras

PEACOCK ORE: equality, justice, independence, strength, healing

PREHNITE: unconditional love, meditation, connected to Archangel Raphael and the extraterrestrial, inner knowledge, prophecies, spiritual growth, peace, protection, harmony with nature, help with nightmares, fears, and phobias

PUMICE: cleansing, cleansing the aura, emotional support during difficult situations

PURPONITE: bringing good luck to your business, money, increasing sales

QUARTZ (BLUE): tranquility, peace, help with bad moods, hope, helping others

QUARTZ (GOLDEN): telepathy, healing

QUARTZ (GREEN): opening and balancing the Heart chakra, creativity, prosperity, success

QUARTZ (HARLEQUIN): connecting the Root and Heart chakras with the Crown chakra, vitality, balance, universal love

QUARTZ (LITHIUM): healing animals and plants, antidepressant, healing past lives' emotional diseases, cleansing all chakras, purifying water

QUARTZ (SMOKY): grounding, raising vibrations during meditation, protection, passion, connection to the Root chakra and Earth, dissolving stress, fear, and negative emotions, help fighting depression

QUARTZ (SPIRIT): raising vibrations, assisting during the transition to another life

QUARTZ (TANGERINE): healing traumas, healing after psychic attacks, past lives healing, activation of the Sacral chakra, positivity

QUARTZ (TIBETAN): carrying the resonance of Tibet and Tibetan people and the esoteric knowledge present in their land, access to the Akashic Records (see page 80), grounding, energizing the aura

RHODONITE: operating against gossip, confidence, balancing emotions, cleansing and activating the Heart chakra and our heart, boosting the power of mantras during meditation, emotional healing, help healing codependency, abuse, and emotional self-destruction

SAPPHIRE: fidelity, complicity in romantic relationships, legal matters, wisdom, calm, serenity, self-expression, concentration, releasing frustration and confusion, help healing depression

SARDONYX: protection from crimes, rituals for the community, strength, protection, lasting happiness, good luck, willpower, alleviation of depression

TOURMALINE (BLACK): protection, protection against psychic attacks, grounding, vitality, positive attitude

TOURMALINE (BLUE): responsibility, truth, loyalty, honesty, activating the Throat and Third Eye chakras, spiritual freedom, self-expression, psychic awareness, love, harmony, releasing sadness

TOURMALINE (BROWN): grounding, clearing our aura, empathy, help solving family problems, understanding between people

TOURMALINE (GREEN): working with herbs and flowers, healing, patience, compassion, transforming negative energies into positive ones, calming the mind

TOURMALINE (YELLOW): sexual revitalization, self-awareness, introspection, spiritual development, purification, balancing emotions, relieving discomfort

TOURMALINE (PINK): love, sex magick, aphrodisiac energies, intimacy, self-love

TOURMALINE (PURPLE): healing the heart, connection to the Root and Heart chakras, creativity, intuition, getting rid of old patterns and pain

TOURMALINE (RAINBOW): imagination, creativity, releasing creative blockages, new ideas

TOURMALINE (RED): helping introverted people in social situations, helping understand love, creativity, healing and charging the Sacral chakra, vitality

TOURMALINE (WATERMELON): activating the Heart chakra, love, friendship, diplomacy, security, self-expression, joy, good in relationships, balance, dissolving old pains, help healing depression

UNAKITE: connection to those who love animals and nature, strengthening the bond with your pet, spirituality, psychic visions, grounding, bringing calm energies to the environment

ZIRCON: Red zircon is used for sex magick, yellow zircon for success in business, green zircon for money magick, and clear zircon can replace diamonds in spells.

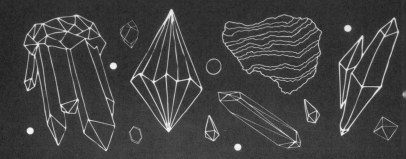

CHAPTER FOUR

SPELLS, RITUALS, AND CRYSTAL GRIDS

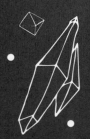

PROSPERITY SPELL JAR

This spell will attract prosperity into your life that could manifest through a job opportunity, success in your business, or other magickal events. You can perform it during a New Moon or on Wednesdays.

GLASS JAR (OF ANY DIMENSION)	GREEN AVENTURINE
	CITRINE
RICE	
	A PIECE OF PAPER WITH YOUR GOAL WRITTEN ON IT
DRIED BASIL	
THYME	

1   Before starting the spell, remember to cleanse all the ingredients. You can cleanse them through visualization, with an incense stick, or whatever cleansing tool best suits you.

2   First place the rice in the glass jar, followed by the herbs. Then place your crystals and the paper, folded three times, into the jar. Based on how big the jar is, you can decide whether to use crystal chips or bigger pieces.

3   Spend some time meditating and focusing on what you'd like to manifest while holding the jar. Imagine your dream as if it has already happened, enjoying every feeling and happy thought.

4   Close the jar and thank all the ingredients for the help they will provide you.

5   You can keep your spell jar on your altar, in your

bag, or anywhere that will allow you to see the jar daily. Shake it when you feel the energies are fading; when you feel you have benefited from all the power that the jar could give, you can open it, cleanse and keep your crystals, and return all the herbs to nature.

LOVE CANDLE SPELL

Candle spells are a common and powerful way to perform magick. The fire of the candle will release all the energies of the ingredients you choose to add, sending your powerful intent into the universe. This candle spell will boost self-love and self-acceptance, reminding you to love yourself first. For this spell, you can use long candles, votive candles, or the jar candles sold in many shops. If you want to give this spell a boost of power, perform it on a Friday night, Aphrodite's favored time of week.

A PINK (OR WHITE) CANDLE

VANILLA ESSENTIAL OIL DILUTED IN A CARRIER OIL

HIBISCUS

CRUSHED ROSE QUARTZ

1   Cleanse all your ingredients with visualization, an incense stick, or whatever cleansing method best suits you.

2   Anoint your candle with the oil mixture. I advise mixing seven drops of essential oil with two

tablespoons of olive oil (feel free to use other carrier oils if you don't like olive oil).

3 Mix the hibiscus with the rose quartz and sprinkle it onto your candle.

4 Light the candle, and while it's burning spend some time meditating on loving yourself and accepting yourself for the amazing being you are.

5 Let the candle burn until the end.*

*IF YOU CAN'T LET THE CANDLE BURN UNTIL THE END, DO NOT LEAVE IT BURNING WITHOUT SUPERVISION. YOU CAN BLOW IT OUT AND LIGHT IT AGAIN WHEN YOU'RE ABLE TO KEEP AN EYE ON IT.

PROTECT AND CLEANSE YOUR HOUSE SPRAY SPELL

Spray spells are very easy to make and you can use them for consecutive days. This is a perfect way to practice magick if you don't have a lot of time and if you feel like you need to perform a spell on a daily basis. This spell will clear your house from unwanted energies and bless it.

A SPRAY BOTTLE

WATER (EVEN BETTER IF IT'S MOON WATER)

DRIED SAGE

DRIED ROSEMARY

CLEAR QUARTZ

A PINCH OF SALT

1 Cleanse all your ingredients with visualization, an incense stick, or whatever cleansing method best suits you.

2 Fill your spray bottle with water.

3 Add your dried herbs, the clear quartz, and a pinch of salt.

4 Infuse your intent; ask the ingredients to get rid of any unwanted energies and bless your home.

5 Close the bottle and spray it in each room that needs the power of the spell.

BODY AND MIND PROTECTION BATH SPELL

Bath spells are probably the most relaxing spells; they provide a moment where you can enjoy some time with yourself and relax while still performing magick. If you don't have a bath, you can still place the ingredients around your shower and enjoy the influence of the herbs on your body. This spell will bring relaxation and peace and will protect you from negative energies.

WHITE SALT   AMETHYST

CANDLES   AGATE

SELENITE

1 Fill your bath with nice warm water and sprinkle some salt in. This will help absorb negative energies.

2 To create a relaxing atmosphere, light some candles (I always like to pick uneven numbers).

3 Position your crystals around you, on the edges of the bath or anywhere near you.

4 Enjoy your bath. Close your eyes and feel the magickal presence of your crystals. Imagine all the stress and negative energies leaving your body, and experience a sense of balance and peace.

5 When you open the drain, imagine the water taking away all the negative energies.

PEACEFUL SLEEP RITUAL

When our mind is full of preoccupations and stress, or after an intense day at work, it might be difficult to relax and have a good night's rest.

This simple ritual will help you prepare your mind and body for bedtime, promoting good rest.

A MUG   WARM WATER

DRIED LAVENDER   1 TEASPOON HONEY

DRIED CHAMOMILE   CELESTITE

1 Cleanse all your ingredients with visualization, an incense stick, or whatever cleansing method best suits you.

2   Put some dried lavender and chamomile in a tea strainer over a mug. Pour in some warm water and let the herbs infuse for five to ten minutes.

3   Add a teaspoon of honey and enjoy your drink while holding a piece of celestite.

4   Before going to bed, repeat this aloud three times: "I will rest peacefully and enjoy my night of sleep."

5   Place celestite near your bed and have a peaceful sleep.

INCREASE YOUR INTUITION AND VISIONS

This is a simple meditation ritual that will help you activate your Third Eye and increase your intuition and visions. You can also practice some yoga in addition to this ritual, specifically to open and activate your sixth chakra.

INCENSE STICK   IOLITE

A YOGA MAT OR A
MEDITATION PILLOW

1   Go to a quiet place where no one can disturb or distract you.

2   Light an incense stick to increase focus and relaxation.

3   Lie down on your yoga mat and place iolite on your Third Eye or sit down on a meditation pillow and hold iolite in your hands.

4   Clear your mind from intrusive thoughts. Spend as

much time as you can focusing on your Third Eye and the iolite's energy.

5 Before ending your meditation session, take a deep breath and express gratitude for the work that was done.

CONNECT TO HIGHER REALMS

Connecting to spirits, higher realms, or our astral self is a great spiritual practice to connect us with our powers, manifest our desires, and receive messages from higher beings that can help us better our existence on this planet.

HEMATITE OR
ANOTHER GROUNDING
STONE

LABRADORITE

SELENITE

1 Find a nice, quiet spot where no one can disturb or distract you.

2 Ground yourself, feel present in the moment, and free your mind from intrusive thoughts. You can use hematite or any other grounding stone for a little help.

3 Hold labradorite in one hand and selenite in the other; go into a meditative state.

4 Imagine lines of lights coming out of the stones, going through your body from your head to the sky and from your feet to underground.

5 Become aware of colors, sounds, and feelings. Feel

the power of the energies that are flowing. Observe what the realms and your higher self have to communicate to you.

6   When you're finished, write down anything you felt, saw, or heard. Maybe it won't make much sense in the moment, but you will eventually find the meaning in the future.

MANIFESTATION BRACELET

This charm will help you boost the energies of your manifestation practice. Wearing it will remind you of your goals and your potential to manifest all your dreams.

QUARTZ BEADS   STRING FOR BEADING

NEBULA STONE BEADS
(USE TIGER'S EYE AS A
SUBSTITUTE)

1   Cleanse all your ingredients with visualization, an incense stick, or whatever cleansing method best suits you.

2   Empower your crystal beads with your intention and ask them to help you manifest your desires.

3   Create your bracelet, measuring the size of string to fit your wrist.

4   While you create your bracelet, repeat: "I ask my spirit guides to assist me in the creating of this

manifestation charm. May it manifest my desires, dreams, and goals, strengthening my powers and guiding me throughout my path. This is my will, so Mote it Be!"

5 Wear your bracelet and be open to seeing what it will have to offer.

FLOWER OF LIFE GRID

CRYSTAL GRID FOR LOVE

Crystal grids are a specific and intentional arrangement of crystals, boosting their collective power in order to manifest your desires. This crystal grid will enhance the love in your current relationship or help you attract a new love. You can create a crystal grid anywhere you want—on your table, altar, or in this case, even under your bed.

It is common to use specific sacred geometric patterns as a "floor" to place your crystals on to enhance the energies and your intention.

It is advised you use at least two different crystal shapes, but don't worry if you don't have them.

ROSE QUARTZ

RHODONITE

CARNELIAN

FLOWER OF LIFE GRID

A PIECE OF PAPER WITH YOUR INTENTION WRITTEN ON IT

QUARTZ OR SELENITE WAND (OPTIONAL)

1 Cleanse all your ingredients with visualization, an incense stick, or whatever cleansing method best suits you.

2 Empower your crystals with your intent and try to keep the focus on what you want to achieve.

3 Place the Flower of Life grid where you'd like to position your crystal grid.

4 Position the paper with your intention in the middle of the grid and put the biggest piece of crystal on top. This will be your master crystal, which will emanate the highest frequency.

5 Place the other crystals, starting from the outside and moving inward. Stay focused on your intention.

6 Activate your grid. You can do this by saying your intention out loud and drawing an imaginary line to connect all your crystals with your finger (you can also do this using a quartz or selenite wand).

CRYSTAL GRID FOR MONEY

This crystal grid is perfect if you're seeking to attract more money into your life. This grid is called the Seed of Life, and it promotes new beginnings, wealth, and fulfilment. If you can't use this grid, you can still use the Flower of Life or decide to do this more freely, without using any sacred geometry.

THE SEED OF LIFE GRID

CITRINE

PYRITE

GREEN JADE

THE SEED OF LIFE GRID

QUARTZ OR SELENITE WAND (OPTIONAL)

1   Cleanse all your ingredients with visualization, an incense stick, or whatever cleansing method best suits you.

2   Empower your crystals with your intent and try to keep the focus on what you want to achieve.

3   Place the grid wherever you'd like in your home.

4 Place the biggest crystal piece in the middle.
   Mindfully place the other crystals. If you're using
   pointed crystals, remember to position them pointing
   inward if you want to attract more money, and out-
   ward if you're sending the energy to someone else.

5 Activate your grid. You can do this by saying your
   intention out loud and drawing an imaginary line to
   connect all your crystals with your finger (you can
   also do this using a quartz or selenite wand).

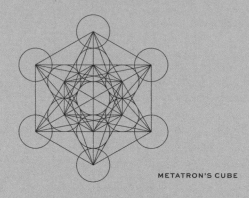

METATRON'S CUBE

CRYSTAL GRID FOR HEALING

This crystal grid is perfect if you want to experience
emotional healing. It will help you dissolve mental
pain and past traumas and bring inner peace. The
grid I use is called Metatron's Cube, which turns
negative thoughts into positive ones and symbolizes
balance and harmony.

METATRON'S CUBE

A PIECE OF PAPER
WITH YOUR GOAL
WRITTEN ON IT

BLUE LACE AGATE

FLUORITE

MALACHITE

QUARTZ OR SELENITE
WAND (OPTIONAL)

1 Cleanse all your ingredients with visualization, an incense stick, or whatever cleansing method best suits you.

2 Empower your crystals with your intent and try to keep the focus on what you want to achieve.

3 Place the grid wherever you'd like in your home.

4 Place your paper, folded three times, in the middle of the grid. Place the biggest piece of crystal on top of it.

5 Place the other crystals inside each circle and in the middle of each line forming the hexagon.

6 Activate your grid. You can do this by saying your intention out loud and drawing an imaginary line to connect all your crystals with your finger (you can also do this using a quartz or selenite wand).

ELIXIR TO BOOST THE IMMUNE SYSTEM

Elixirs are waters infused with the energies of one or more crystals.

Nowadays, you can find ready-made bottles containing crystals in stores. However, you can still make your personal mixture at home. Please, always do your research and make sure to use crystals that are not toxic or poisonous when in contact with water. This is an antioxidant elixir, perfect to support our health and keep us hydrated.

WATER   SAGE

ELDERFLOWER   A CUP

GINGER   CLEAR QUARTZ

1 Cleanse all your ingredients with visualization, an incense stick, or whatever cleansing method best suits you.

2 Boil some water while you place elderflower, ginger, and sage in a cup.

3 Pour the hot water into the cup and let the herbs infuse for at least ten minutes.

4 When the water starts cooling down, add the clear quartz.

5 Infuse your intent; you can then drink it or sprinkle it around.

CREATIVITY ELIXIR

This elixir will stimulate your brain, increase your creativity, and bring new ideas. Drink it before starting a creative activity or before work.

WATER

ASHWAGANDHA (ROOT
OR POWDER)

TURMERIC

A CUP

BLOODSTONE

1   Cleanse all your ingredients with visualization, an incense stick, or whatever cleansing method best suits you.

2   Boil some water while you place Ashwagandha and turmeric in a cup.

3   Pour the hot water into the cup and let the herbs infuse for at least ten minutes.

4   When the water starts cooling down, add the bloodstone.

5   Infuse your intent; you can then drink it or sprinkle it around.

ELIXIR FOR PLANTS

This elixir is an excellent gift to give to your plants when you're watering them. It will help them grow and store some positive energy.

WATER

MINT

CINNAMON

A SPRAY BOTTLE

MOSS AGATE

TOURMALINE

1   Cleanse all your ingredients with visualization, an incense stick, or whatever cleansing method best suits you.

2   Boil some water while you place mint and cinnamon in a spray bottle.

3   Pour the hot water into the spray bottle and let the herbs infuse for at least ten minutes.

4   When the water starts cooling down, add the moss agate and tourmaline. Allow the water to cool completely.

5   Infuse your intent; spray it on your plants daily.

CONCLUSION

With this book, I wanted to share the importance of taking care of our spiritual body as well as our physical one; this practice is precious to me. Without a healthy mind and nurtured soul, we cannot reach our full potential as magickal beings. That is why the best healing practice starts with loving ourselves and others every single day. By doing so we set off on the path toward wisdom and unconditional love.

Crystals embody this philosophy and way of living, connecting us not only to our inner self but to other people and higher realms.

I hope that after reading this book, you will find the crystals that are meant to accompany you on this beautiful journey full of connections and healing.

May your path be surrounded by magick, happiness, and love, and may your crystals always be with you.

BLESSED BE!

ISABELLA FERRARI was born and raised in Italy. After living for more than two years at ILTK, the acclaimed Buddhist institute, she became a meditation teacher. She then lived in London for a few years to explore her interest in music and art. She is the author of *Witchcraft Simplified*, *Tarot Simplified*, and the novel *Ocean Crayon*, and wrote for her own website and many important magazines as a music journalist. Her passion for spirituality and religions inspired her to deeply study the different branches of Paganism and create her project Greenwitchcom. Find her on Instagram @greenwitchcom.

ABOUT CIDER MILL PRESS BOOK PUBLISHERS

Good ideas ripen with time. From seed to harvest, Cider Mill Press brings fine reading, information, and entertainment together between the covers of its creatively crafted books. Our Cider Mill bears fruit twice a year, publishing a new crop of titles each spring and fall.

"Where Good Books Are Ready for Press"

Visit us online at
cidermillpress.com

or write to us at
501 Nelson Place
Nashville, TN 37214